A FUTURE FOR THE NHS? HEALTH CARE IN THE 1990s

A Future for the NHS?
Health Care in the 1990s

Wendy Ranade

LONGMAN
London and New York

Longman Group Limited
Longman House, Burnt Mill,
Harlow, Essex CM20 2JE, England
and Associated Companies throughout the world.

*Published in the United States of America
by Longman Publishing, New York*

© Longman Group UK Limited 1994

First published 1994
Third impression 1995
ISBN 0582 05978X PPR

British Library Cataloguing-in-Publication Data

A catalogue record for this book is available from the British Library

Library of Congress Cataloging-in-Publication Data
Ranade, Wendy, 1940–
    A future for the NHS? : health care in the 1990s / Wendy Ranade.
        p.   cm.
    Includes bibliographical references and index.
    ISBN 0-582-05978-X
    1. National Health Service (Great Britain) 2. Medical care–
    –Political aspects—Great Britain. 3. Medical care–Great Britain–
    –Forecasting.   I. Title.
RA412.5.G7R35 1993   93 14037
362. 1'0941--dc20   CIP

Set in Times
Produced through Longman Malaysia, CLP

CONTENTS

FIGURES AND TABLES

ABBREVIATIONS

BMA	British Medical Association
CHC	Community Health Council
DGH	District General Hospital
DGM	District General Manager
DOH	Department of Health
DHA	District Health Authority
DHSS	Department of Health and Social Security
DMU	District Managed Unit
FHSA	Family Health Services Authority
GDP	Gross Domestic Product
GP	General Practitioner
GPFH	General Practitioner Fundholders
HFA	Health for All
HCHS	Hospital and Community Health Service
HMO	Health Maintenance Organisation
NAHA	National Association of Health Authorities
NAHAT	National Association of Health Authorities and Trusts
NHSME	National Health Service Management Executive
OECD	Organisation for Economic Cooperation and Development
QALY	Quality-adjusted life year
RAWP	Resource Allocation Working Party
RGM	Regional General Manager
SMR	Standardised mortality ratio
TQM	Total quality management
UGM	Unit general manager
WHO	World Health Organisation
WFP	*Working for Patients*

ACKNOWLEDGEMENTS

My biggest thanks go to my wonderful husband Palu, for his unfailing support and all the delicious meals he cooked to keep up my morale. Thanks to Mary Mellor for reading the whole manuscript from the perspective of a good writer from a different academic discipline, and to Arthur Walker for his helpful comments on Chapters 4 and 5. To Graeme Duncan, Head of the Department of Economics and Government, University of Northumbria, for being helpful and understanding about the pressures of writing this book and coping with a large research project at the same time. To the research team in the Monitoring Managed Competition project, John Appleby, Val Little, Ray Robinson and Paula Smith, and the managers and clinicians who took part, as well as my colleagues in Newcastle Health Authority whom I was privileged to work with as a non-executive member. I learnt a good deal about the health service and about management from them all. To the librarians at the University of Northumbria, particularly Austin McArthy and Graham Walton for being so helpful. Finally to all the students from health and social welfare I have enjoyed teaching over the years, particularly on the Diploma and M.Sc. course in Health and Social Research, and the M.Sc. course in Strategy and Resource Management. They provided vital insights into the day-to-day realities of life in the NHS and brought flights of fancy firmly back to earth.

CHAPTER 1

Introduction

The health care systems of many countries throughout the developed world are being reformed and restructured. The changes taking place are manifested in diverse forms, and have very different starting points, but underlying them are similar sets of questions and pressures.

How can health services be restructured to meet the needs of ageing populations more appropriately? How can the difference between the possible and the affordable in health care be resolved, as medical advance continues to widen the gap? What should the division be between public and private spending on health care, and can publicly funded systems continue to offer a comprehensive range of services? What are the ethics of different ways of rationing health care? How can doctors be made more accountable for the resources they use and what kind of incentives are appropriate? How relevant are medical definitions of health to current health problems?

In the current ferment of change and experimentation, the British National Health Service is in the forefront. A pioneering concept in 1948, the NHS remained the prime example of a centrally planned and funded public health service. In 1990 it again pioneered a new model of organising and delivering health services by introducing a 'quasi-market' or managed competition: creating a structure of buyers and sellers by separating responsibility for the purchase of health care from its provision, and allowing limited competition for business between providers – hospitals, community health services, ambulance services, and so on – within strict regulatory guidelines. Several other countries, such as Sweden, Finland, New Zealand and some of the new democracies of Eastern Europe, are experimenting with their own versions of this hybrid development.

In Britain the reforms which were introduced in the White Paper *Working for Patients* in 1989 were never widely understood and have still not won public support. Within the NHS many staff were bewildered, confused and deeply worried about their implications. This book draws on the author's experience of teaching health policy for many years to health service practitioners, and a keen awareness of how successive 'reorganisations' appear to those delivering patient care in hospital wards and in the community. Changes can appear (often with good reason) to have no sense or logic, confined to relatively remote tiers of management and far from the real business of caring for patients.

The book therefore has two aims. The first is to locate what is happening in the NHS to a broader ideological, economic, social and political context, and the second is to explain in some detail how the reforms have been implemented and what their current status is. Its starting premise is the need for a wider debate among the public on the kinds of questions raised above, which at present is conducted within fairly narrow health circles.

If previous experience is any guide, politicians cannot be relied on to lead that debate. When the NHS grabs the headlines, which it characteristically does at election times, the arguments rarely get beyond statistical claims and counter claims on the issue of 'underfunding', or charges of sinister intent which are met with protestations of undying fealty to the 'principles' of the NHS. (In the 1992 election it hardly got beyond a slanging match over who had identified the young patient awaiting treatment for glue ear who was featured in a Labour election broadcast.) Debates about what a modern health care system can be expected to provide, how limited resources can be used to best effect and what needs to be done in a broader sense to improve the health of the population are edged to the margins or never addressed. The 'principles' of the NHS are equated with a particular set of institutional arrangements which, like a sanctified ancient monument, cannot be touched but continue to crumble away under the onslaught of wind and weather.

Round and round the mulberry bush

The present reorganisation of the NHS, heralded by the White Paper *Working for Patients* in 1989, marks another attempt to grapple with basic tensions which arise from its organisational form. Klein (1989) argues that the NHS tries to square two circles. First it tries to reconcile central funding and government accountability for national standards of service with the need for local autonomy to meet local need. The result has been a policy see-saw, with governments alternating between periods of centralisation, the better to gain control, followed by a decentralising reaction against the rigidities which are caused as a consequence.

The second tension results from the compact struck between government and the medical profession in 1948, which balanced central accountability for raising and allocating finance with clinical freedom to spend it. The demand for health care (and the resources it consumes) is shaped not just by patients but by a million clinical decisions of doctors and other professionals. As new treatments and technologies proliferate and new needs are identified these demands escalate, but even as early as 1954, the then Minister for Health,

Enoch Powell, discovered that it became a 'positive ethical duty for (providers) to beseige and bombard the government and force or shame them into providing more money . . . and then more again' (Powell 1966). An irresistible force constantly clashes with an immovable object, leading to periodic political 'crises' on the funding issue, and these reached a peak before the 1987 election. Provider power to shape the service also means that the NHS has been unresponsive to central policy direction and strategic planning. A good illustration of this was the vain attempt to give priority to the 'Cinderella' services such as mental illness and mental handicap throughout the 1960s and 1970s.

There have been four attempts to grapple with these tensions through restructuring or internal reorganisation. The 1974 re-organisation was based on the twin principles of rational planning and efficient management, although what was finally brought into being achieved neither. Rational planning was to be achieved by unifying health services, which were at that time split between local authorities, the boards of governors of teaching hospitals, a regional and local administration responsible for other hospitals and the executive councils who administered the contracts for general practitioners (see Figure 1.1).

When proposals for reorganisation were first mooted by a Labour government in 1968, the future structure of local government was also being considered by the Redcliffe-Maud Commission (1969). Ministers believed the Commission would recommend 40–50 local authorities, hence the possibility of creating a matching 40–50 area health boards as a single tier of health service administration. Coherent planning and coordination of health and social care would be facilitated by coterminous boundaries between the two authorities.

In the event, the number of local authorities that emerged with social service responsibilities was nearer 90. Keeping the principle of coterminous boundaries meant 90 health authorities, varying widely in population size. But 90 was thought to be too many to be easily controlled from the centre, which meant retaining the existing tier of regional administration as an executive arm of government, while the variation in population size was tackled by creating a third tier of management in large areas: the district. Driven by the original criterion of coterminosity a highly bureaucratic structure was being created.

The original management proposals were also changed out of recognition. In the 1968 (Ministry of Health 1968) proposals, the boards were envisaged as operating as small executive management teams, with the senior administrator acting as managing director and with far less professional and medical input into decision-making. The syndicalist nature of the NHS, however, forced a number of compromises: a plethora of professional advisory and consultative machinery at every level, and the inclusion of medical and nursing representatives on management teams and health authorities. The end

Figure 1.1 **Structure of NHS 1948–74**

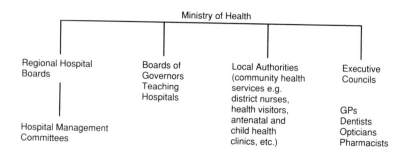

Figure 1.2 **Structure of NHS 1974–82**

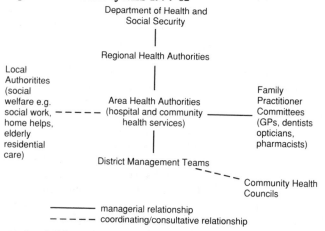

result of this series of political compromises and adjustments, which the Conservatives implemented in 1974, was a seriously flawed structure which certainly could not deliver the government's stated intention of 'maximum accountability upward, maximum delegation downwards' (DHSS 1972) (see Figure 1.2).

Within two years the new Labour government found it necessary to appoint a Royal Commission to investigate the arrangements the Conservatives had put in place, and review the organisation of the NHS once more. Maurice Kogan, whose team at Brunel University undertook a survey of staff attitudes for the Commission found that:

There was a great deal of anger and frustration at what many regard as a seriously over-elaborate system of government, administration and decision-making. The multiplicity of levels, the over-elaboration of consultative machinery, the inability to get decision-making completed nearer the point of delivery of services and what some describe as unacceptably wasteful use of manpower resources were recurrent themes in most of the areas where we worked.

(Merrison Commission 1979: 313)

As a result of the Merrison Commission's recommendations the incoming administration, once again Conservative and headed by Margaret Thatcher, decided on another reorganisation (DHSS 1979), to be carried out in 1982, based on a new set of principles – small is beautiful, with the devolution of decision-making as close as possible to the patient. Coterminosity was abandoned and Area Health Authorities were abolished. Their constituent districts were rearranged into 192 district health authorities, and the 14 regional health authorities retained as a strategic planning tier (see Figure 1.3). The professional advisory machinery was pruned and the planning system simplified, although the composition of health authorities and management stayed intact. The balance had once more swung from centralisation to decentralisation, but the attempt to make doctors and nurses more accountable for resource decisions continued.

Figure 1.3 **Structure of NHS 1982–90**

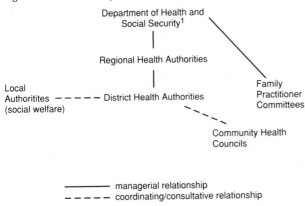

Note:
[1]The Department of Health and Social Security was broken down into two departments again in 1988

Yet the new balance began to be questioned almost as soon as it was in place, this time by Parliamentary committees. The new planning system adopted in 1981 had moved away from detailed prescriptive national targets to relatively broad outlines of central government priorities, more advisory in intent.

Realistically the DHSS had acknowledged the infinite diversity of local circumstances and the reality of local power to shape the implementation of government policy. But this made the Department and ministers once again vulnerable to charges of abdicating their responsibilities for financial and policy goals. In response to criticism from both the Public Accounts Committee and Social Services Committee the Department began to develop new ways of trying to achieve the elusive balance between central accountability and local autonomy and bring the management of health care resources under more effective control.

In 1983 the creation of a new general management function was recommended by a business adviser, Sir Roy Griffiths, and almost immediately implemented. This led to further changes in management structures and processes but also represented a significant challenge to professional power to determine priorities. The current reforms are in many ways a logical development and strengthening of the Griffiths management philosophy, but the nub of the reforms – the creation of the quasi-market – is a radical new departure.

Contents and omissions

Chapter 2 traces the development of the NHS from the perspective of a changing intellectual climate. The political and ideological ideas which shaped the creation of the NHS came under increasingly fierce attack in the 1970s. In part this reflected the wider 'crisis of legitimacy' affecting the welfare state in Britain and many other Western countries and is part of that critique. But it also reflected more specific arguments about the goals of health policy, the role and function of medicine and the power of the medical profession.

Chapter 3 examines some of the larger trends in society which have major significance for health care in general and the NHS in particular, looking in turn at the effects of economic re-structuring, demographic change and technological and medical advance.

Chapter 4 looks at the development of Conservative health policy throughout the 1980s, after the 1982 structure was put in place and up to the publication of the 1989 White Paper *Working for Patients*.

Chapter 5 deals with the implementation of the NHS reforms, concentrating on the theory and practice of 'managed competition'. This and later chapters draw on research findings from a research project undertaken by the author together with colleagues in the National Association of Health Authorities and Trusts, and the Health Service Management Centre, University of Birmingham, on 'Monitoring Managed Competition'. This is one of seven research projects sponsored by the Kings' Fund Institute which are monitoring the reforms over a three-year period.

Changing the style and responsibilities of health service managers has been an important theme of Conservative health policy. Chapter 6 appraises this development within the context of similar changes throughout the public sector and the challenges facing managers in future. Chapter 7 looks at another important theme of the health service reforms – the search for 'quality' in health care. What does this really mean, and is the current fashion for quality merely rhetorical gloss or does it have more substance?

Chapter 8 charts an alternative strategic vision for health policy based on the 'new public health' and the World Health Organisation's strategy of Health for All 2000. Finally, Chapter 9 reviews the strategic context within which health policy choices have to be made in future and the current status of the health service reforms. It concludes by suggesting that the reforms are now at a critical stage but there are ways forward which could take us further on the road to Health for All, if we are prepared to take them.

I regret not being able to deal with the subject of community care policy as extensively as its importance deserves, although there is a general discussion in Chapter 3. This really requires a book in its own right, which would be more useful when there is some experience of implementation to draw on. (The community care aspects of the NHS and Community Care Act 1990 are only being fully implemented from April 1993.) I have no doubt that there are many colleagues more expert than I am on this subject already planning their drafts!

References

Department of Health (1989) *Working for Patients*, Cmnd. 555, London: HMSO.

Department of Health and Social Security (1972) *National Health Service Reorganisation: England*, Cmnd. 5055, London: HMSO.

Department of Health and Social Security and Welsh Office (1979) *Patients first: Consultative Paper on the Structure and Management of The National Health Service in England and Wales*, London: HMSO.

Klein, R. (1989) *The Politics of the NHS*, 2nd edn, London: Longman.

Ministry of Health (1968) *National Health Service: The Administrative Structure of the Medical and Related Services in England and Wales*, London: HMSO.

Powell, J. E. (1966) *Medicine in Politics*, London: Pitman Medical.

Royal Commission on Local Government in England (1969) Cmnd. 4040 *The Redcliffe-Maud Report*, London: HMSO.

Royal Commission on the National Health Service (1979) Cmnd. 7615 *The Merrison Report*, London: HMSO.

CHAPTER 2

The ideological context

Health policy can only be understood within the context of the ideas and values which have shaped its development historically. This chapter looks at the main academic and political perspectives on health and health care which have shaped the debate, and revolves around three broad areas of analysis. First, how health and illness are to be defined and what their determinants are; second, the values underpinning the structuring and organisation of health care; and third the function and power of medicine in modern society and the role of the medical profession within it.

Different perspectives also have a chronological dimension. Historically the Fabian socialist perspective dominated the development of social policy in Britain from the end of the Second World War to the mid-1970s and contributed powerfully to the rationale underpinning a free, comprehensive, universal and state-provided health service. Klein argues that the remarkable political consensus that existed on these principles in 1948 was accompanied by an even more profound consensus about the benefits of medicine and what it could achieve.

> . . . this mirrored the belief that medical science had not only triumphed over disease and illness in the past but would continue to do so in future. On this view, the only problem was how best to create an institutional framework which would bring the benefits of medical science more efficiently and equitably to the people of Britain.
>
> (Klein 1989: 27)

In the 1970s optimism and faith gave way to disillusion and doubt as medical costs soared with little apparent benefit. Even the past successes of medicine were challenged as illusory, and the role and power of the medical profession were subject to a number of influential critiques. While certain of the criticisms made then are now widely accepted even within the medical profession itself, no new consensus has yet emerged on the goals of health policy or the principles which should govern its organisation and distribution.

Inevitably a brief account cannot do justice to individual writers and exaggerates the extent of agreement within each broad perspective, but it does emphasise central points of similarity and difference.

The social-democratic consensus

The founding of the NHS was one of the key acts of the 1945 Attlee Government which laid the foundations of the postwar accord on the welfare state, full employment and the managed mixed economy. Built on the economic foundations of Keynesian economics and the social policy prescriptions of the Beveridge Report, the accord bridged the 'reluctant collectivists' in the Conservative party (George and Wilding 1976), concerned with the survival and prosperity of capitalism, and the Fabian socialists in the Labour party trying to transform it from within.

Socialist proposals for state-provided health care can be traced back to the Webbs' Minority Report of the Royal Commission on the Poor Law in 1905. The medical profession itself, notably in the Dawson Report of 1920, advocated some kind of comprehensive health care provision for the whole population. The fragmentation and inequities of prewar arrangements were highlighted in 1937 by an influential report from the Department of Political and Economic Planning but it took the Second World War and the Beveridge Report of 1942 to change perceptions sufficiently to legitimise a greatly enhanced role for the state in the provision of health care. Beveridge provided a rationale based on concepts of national efficiency, rationality and the rights of citizenship. As a Liberal, Beveridge falls into the 'reluctant collectivist' camp but his proposals received enthusiastic endorsement from leading Fabians and show the influence of their ideas. In particular his concern with social benefit and social cost (the costs of ill-health fall on the community, not just the individual), the view that welfare spending should be regarded as a social investment which could increase national productivity and efficiency and his technocratic approach to solving social problems are all typically Fabian.

Klein (1989) argues that the same emphasis on efficiency and administrative rationality characterised internal Labour party debates on the final shape and form of the service and went hand in hand with their commitment to equity and equality. In spite of his radical socialist image and his furious battles with the medical profession over implementation, Bevan's vision of the health service was essentially paternalist. Health knowledge resided with the 'experts', essentially the medical profession, and this won doctors a privileged place in administering the new system, denied to other professional groups. The effect was to 'medicalise' large areas of health policy and define them as off-limits to lay influence.

It also led to the creation of a lopsided system in line with the structure of medical priorities and values. Curative, hospital-based medicine dominated at the expense of prevention, health promotion and community services, and high priority was given to the treatment of short-term episodes of acute illness to the detriment of the care and rehabilitation of the chronically ill. Although both Beveridge and

Bevan had acknowledged the superiority of prevention over cure, the design of the new system ensured that it remained underdeveloped. By privileging medicine in the administration of the new service, separating hospitals from local authority responsibilities for prevention and after care, and leaving the power and independence of the teaching hospitals intact, Bevan created a medical service not a health service. Restoring the balance between prevention, cure and care has been a major or minor theme of health policy ever since. It figures prominently as an objective of current policy for the health service, and is a major theme of this book.

The Fabian model of welfare

Fabians continued to dominate the study of social policy throughout the 1950s and 1960s, developing a welfare model which had a powerful influence on policy-makers and contributed to a shared perspective between academics, civil servants and politicians on the role of the state in social policy. Essentially this was based on optimistic views about social progress and economic growth. Welfare spending, it was argued, aided economic development in three main ways. It stabilised demand by income transfers to those who had a high propensity to consume. This in turn contributed to the maintenance of full employment. Finally welfare spending, particularly on education and health, improved the quality and productivity of labour. If welfare aided economic growth it was also dependent on it. Crosland (1956) argued that economic growth was essential if the Fabian strategy of equality was to succeed. A growing national income would ease the political and social difficulties of redistribution and allow the provision of more generous social benefits which would help to equalise consumption patterns.

  Fabians also believed that public welfare had a vital role to play in integrating society, alleviating social conflict and promoting the expression of altruistic sentiments countering, if partially, the atomism, selfishness and inequalities of capitalist market economies. Integration was a strong theme in the work of Richard Titmuss. In words which betray the influence of functionalist sociology, Titmuss wrote: 'social policy . . . manifests society's will to survive as an organic whole . . . and is centred (on) those institutions which encourage integration and discourage alienation' (Titmuss 1963: 39). The universal and comprehensive nature of the health service enshrined these principles more perfectly than any other social service.

  Harris (1987) points out that Fabian academics of this generation were almost unfailingly hostile to market-based welfare systems. Underlying this hostility was a profound belief in the ethical and moral superiority of collective welfare provision. Probably Bevan himself expressed this most eloquently in relation to health care:

The field in which the claims of individual commercialism come into most immediate conflict with reputable notions of social values is that of health . . . no society can legitimately call itself civilized if a sick person is denied medical aid because of lack of means . . . Society becomes more wholesome, more serene and spiritually healthier, if it knows that its citizens have at the back of their consciousness the knowledge that not only themselves, but all their fellows have access when ill, to the best that medical skill can provide.

(Bevan 1961: 98–100)

In the next 20 years the NHS did not escape criticism from academic Fabians but it never reached the volume and intensity of the criticism which, for example, social security and income maintenance attracted as they appeared to retreat further and further away from the principles of the Beveridge Report.

Challenging the mystique of medicine

The optimistic consensus on medicine which had helped to sustain high and growing health expenditures in the Western world throughout the 1960s began to dissolve in the 1970s. Medicine's achievements and potential were put under the microscope and re-evaluated more critically. The power and function of the medical profession were subject to a disparate but intense attack.

The roots of disillusion lay in the widening gap between medicine's claims and its achievements. As one set of health problems was eliminated in developed countries (the infectious diseases), another more difficult and intractable set was revealed. Medicine seemed to be able, at best, to alleviate the growing burden of degenerative and chronic illness: arthritis, diabetes, respiratory disease, and mental illnesses like schizophrenia or Alzheimer's disease. Survivors of serious accidents or genetic handicap at birth could be kept alive, but often for a lifetime of expensive treatment and care. Many of the principal modern causes of mortality and morbidity – coronary heart disease, most cancers, stroke, accidents – were difficult and expensive to treat and resistant to cure. Consequently 1940s' optimism about a finite amount of ill-health and disease susceptible to a comprehensive health care system was seen to be false, based on erroneous concepts of health and illness. Far from being static these are redefined over time in line with economic and social change.

Wrestling with inequalities

Equally important in undermining the hopes of egalitarians in Britain was growing evidence of persistent inequalities between the classes in health status in spite of 30 years of a free health service. Reviewing the evidence in 1980 the Black Report (DHSS 1980) concluded that at every stage of the life-cycle there was a substantial class gradient in mortality and that class differences had remained comparatively stable since 1930. Self-reported illness, sickness absence rates and a growing number of studies on specific aspects of ill-health all supported the main conclusion: the greatest burden of ill-health and disability was borne by the worst off.

In part this was attributed to inequalities in access and utilisation. The NHS had inherited a gross geographical maldistribution of facilities in 1948 which meant that in practice 'equality of access' was a chimera. Progress was made on certain aspects of the problem (for example, the distribution of general practitioners and underprovided specialities like psychiatry and anaesthesia), but by 1970 Tudor Hart could still proclaim the truth of the 'inverse care law': 'The availability of good medical care tends to vary inversely with the need for it in the population served' (Hart 1971: 405–12).

The evidence on uptake was more mixed although there was a clear class gradient with regard to preventive services. Higher social groups appeared to make more use of health services in relation to need however (Brotherston 1976; Forster 1976) and research published shortly after the Black Report argued that they also obtained a disproportionate share of NHS resources when ill (Le Grand 1982).

The authors of the Black Report, who included one of the most eminent Fabian academics, Professor Peter Townsend, were clear that such disparities were socially unjust and the NHS needed policies to address them, but they were forced to conclude from the evidence that the major causes of health inequalities lay beyond the NHS and were rooted in the material conditions of life experienced by the different classes. Inequalities in health simply reflected wider structures of economic and social inequality which health care was powerless to redress. The Fabian 'strategy for equality' through redistributing services in kind appeared to have failed. (Although failure is relative: the welfare services may have contained inequalities and prevented them from getting worse.)

The McKeown thesis

Medicine's growing number of critics were given important empirical support by the work of Thomas McKeown, which exposed not only its present limitations but threw doubt on its past successes. McKeown published *The Modern Rise of Population and the Role of Medicine* in 1976 as an accessible summary of two decades of painstaking work, applying the insights of medical and epidemiological knowledge to a historical analysis of Britain's detailed national series of death records, which began in 1847.

McKeown's main purpose was to take away from scientific

medicine any credit for the decline in mortality which took place in England and Wales in the nineteenth century. He did so by demonstrating conclusively that many of the most important diseases involved had virtually disappeared before the relevant medical innovations had occurred. He also had an alternative explanation: the major factor responsible was rising standards of living, of which the most significant feature was improved diet (McKeown 1976). Improved public health and hygiene measures – the 'sanitary revolution' from the mid-years of the century – were also important and eliminated up to one-quarter of deaths between then and 1971.

McKeown's attack on the 'medical model' of health was shared by critics from radical, feminist and Marxist perspectives.

The radical critique

The radical critique has originated both from within medicine, particularly epidemiology, and from sociology. The first exposes the limitations of modern medical practice, often exposing its claims to scientific status as dubious. Cochrane (1971) for example, argued that medicine has a poor record of evaluative research: fashion, whim and personal preference often dictate the choice of a particular procedure, and many common interventions are unvalidated, of proven ineffectiveness or produce iatrogenic illness (illness caused as a result of medical intervention).

The sociological variant combines similar scepticism with an analysis of medical power and its effects and is based on a wider critique of the professions and professionalism. An early and influential contribution was Eliot Freidson's *Professional Dominance* and *The Profession of Medicine* (1970a; 1970b). Freidson argued that the 'analytical key' to understanding the organisation of health services and their inadequacies was the professional dominance of medicine at the apex of an elaborate division of labour. Other health care professions are subordinate to the organised autonomy of doctors who claim sole rights of diagnosis and treatment. Freidson analyses how medicine has acquired these monopoly legal and political rights from the state, and the consequences of this for patients. Building on this work John Ehrenreich argues that the cultural practices and values of Western medicine and inequalities of power between doctor and patient lead to the production of a racist, sexist, harmful and ineffective medical system (Ehrenreich 1978).

The most damning and best-known indictment of medicine in the radical tradition is *Medical Nemesis* by Ivan Illich. Centring his discussion on an analysis of present patterns of mortality Illich argues that medicine is not only ineffective but causes positive damage (iatrogenesis) at three levels. Damage and suffering are inflicted on patients in the course of clinical treatment as a result of 'the undesirable side effects of approved, mistaken, callous or contra-indicated technical contacts with the medical system . . .' (Illich 1976: 26). Second, the 'medicalisation of life' destroys people's capacity for self-care and self-responsibility. Illich claims that doctors have done much to mystify the public about the real causes of ill-health and fostered the illusion of miracle cures for every ill – if enough money is spent looking for them. We are all turned into addicts of medicine as every stage of human life from pregnancy and childbirth to old age and dying becomes colonised and labelled by medicine. 'Life turns from a succession of different stages of health into a series of periods each requiring different therapies' (ibid 1976: 44). At an even deeper level medicine destroys a people's ability to deal with their own vulnerability and weakness in an autonomous and personal way by attacking traditional cultural values, routines and rituals which allowed individuals to make meaningful the universal human experience of pain, suffering and death.

Radical solutions to the problems outlined differ. Those who, like Ehrenreich, acknowledge the utility of medical science, want to decontaminate its practice by changing the class, sex and racial composition of medical personnel and promoting a cultural revolution in medical institutions to 'purify' them and instil new values. Since Illich sees only harm in the entire medical enterprise, however, he rejects solutions to democratise or control medical practice or equalise the distribution of medical care. Instead he argues that the whole enterprise of scientific medicine needs to be destroyed as part of a wider de-bureaucratisation and deindustrialisation of modern society to enable more autonomous modes of organisation to develop.

Feminist perspectives

The starting point for feminist analyses of health care is the assumption that the practices and institutions of modern medicine control and disempower women both as consumers and producers of health care, and are unresponsive to their needs.

Feminists of all persuasions distrust the medical model of health, with its mechanistic and individualistic bias. Unlike radicals, however, they do not see medical power resting solely on the dominance of an autonomous profession or the control of highly valued science. (On the contrary, feminists would argue that 'value' is accorded to medical science because men control it.) Through an analysis of gender relations in medicine and health care feminists have related medical power to wider structures of male domination which medicine both reflects and helps to sustain.

In their historical analyses of the development of scientific medicine, feminists have shown how women as the natural (but necessarily unqualified) healers and carers of the sick were displaced by men through a misogynist alliance of Church, state and universities after centuries of struggle (Ehrenreich and English 1979). This ensured that the practice of medicine was based on possession of a university education, from which women were barred. The Church denounced nonprofessional healing as heresy (hence condemning many female midwives to the stake as witches in the fifteenth and sixteenth centuries) and the state was prevailed on to grant a final legal monopoly of practice to the medically qualified by the establishment of the Medical Register in 1858.

The nineteenth and twentieth centuries saw the final triumph of scientific medicine under male control. In the process earlier holistic concepts of healing associated with women healers were eclipsed by an atomistic approach which reduced patients to no more than their dysfunctioning parts.[1] Women re-entered the healthcare arena in the subordinate role of nurses in Florence Nightingale's reorganised profession for 'respectable' ladies in a relationship with medicine which paralleled the patriarchal structure of the bourgeois family, as a quotation from a nursing journal at the turn of the century makes clear:

Women are peculiarly fitted for the onerous task of patiently and skilfully caring for the patient in faithful obedience to the physician's orders. Ability to care for the helpless is women's distinctive nature. Grown up folks when very sick are all babies.

(quoted in Garnikov 1978: 110)

Feminist writers have shown how, both historically and today, women's experience of mental and physical ill-health is related to social causes, with its roots in the inequalities of power they experience in marriage, the family and the labour market. They agree with radicals like Illich that modern medical ideologies mask these realities since 'one of the functions of modern medicine is to call unhappiness disease and locate its cause in the unhappy individual not the diseased social system' (Oakley 1983: 106). However, women are the principal victims of this process since embedded in medical ideologies are gender ideologies which label, stereotype and devalue women.

Feminists have paid particular attention to the way in which an ideology which assigns a primary role to women as mothers informs medical control of reproduction. Through a detailed analysis of contraception, abortion, pregnancy and childbirth, infertility treatment and the menopause they have shown how medicine reinforces and sustains wider structures of male domination over women, through the family and the state. Gender ideologies also assign to women a primary role as carers of the sick, disabled and elderly. Feminist analyses have documented the effects of this: the huge if hidden economic contribution made by the unpaid labour of carers and the financial, emotional and physical costs to the individual.

Feminist solutions to the problems they diagnose depend partly on their theoretical perspective, partly on the specific features of the health policy arena they face in different countries. But whatever their theoretical standpoint, in practice British feminists have had to confront the near monopoly position of the NHS as a provider of services and its role as a massive employer of female labour. They have worked for change within it by, for example, the formation of feminist groups of health workers and professionals, campaigns for more woman-centred services, promoting equal opportunity policies for employees and campaigns to protect abortion rights.

The Marxist critique

The Marxist position starts from the premise that modern medicine must be seen as part of the capitalist mode of production. State involvement in health care in capitalist societies stems from capital's need to reproduce both labour power and the existing social relations of production which ensures the continued dominance of the bougeoisie at an economic, political and ideological level.

State expenditure on health services is directed towards both of these ends. It assists the production of social capital by helping to maintain and reproduce a healthy, productive and pliant labour force. It helps to maintain the legitimacy of existing social relations by relieving suffering and distress, promoting social harmony and caring for nonworking groups. However, the class struggle is played out in medicine as in every other institution of society. The form and organisation of health services in a particular country partly reflects that struggle, hence 'socialised medicine' as in the British health service reflects the organised strength of the working class and their struggle for better health care.

As one of the most influential Marxist analysts of health care, Navarro (1986) argues that working-class people have struggled for medical services not because they are 'mystified' by medicine's bogus claims, as Illich argues, but because it has brought genuine benefits which Illich overlooks, particularly in the care and relief of chronic illness. Hence medicine under capitalism has a dual function, both liberating and controlling. The main difference between the radical and Marxist positions revolves around the issue of medical power. Radicals attribute this to the control of an autonomous medical science and knowledge, Marxists to the class position and function of doctors within capitalism. For Marxists, the changing nature of capitalist interests ultimately dictates what happens in medicine even though doctors themselves may oppose the changes. An example of current importance is the growing corporatisation of health care in the United States which, it is argued, has major implications for the status and autonomy of doctors (McKinlay and Stoeckle 1988).

Similarly, the seemingly autonomous development of medical science has been shaped within a capitalist system of values which sees individuals primarily as producers and in which health is defined largely in terms of restoring the individual's 'fitness' to perform his or her social roles as worker, mother or carer. It is therefore hardly surprising to Marxists that Western medicine has been more interested in curative services for the most productive groups and that nonproductive groups like the disabled, mentally ill and handicapped are less well served.

The emphasis on the individual in medical science also camouflages the real causes of ill-health which are rooted in capitalist economic and social structures – poverty, unemployment, pollution, stressful and unsafe working conditions – the costs of which are borne primarily by the working class and help to explain the stability of class inequalities in health status.

As the ineffectiveness of curative medicine is increasingly exposed (and costs soar) Western medicine has paid more attention to prevention, but again within a narrowly individualistic framework. Once again, Marxists claim, medicine performs its camouflage trick for capitalism, masking the extent to which ill-health originates from the exploitation of workers in the production process itself. The possession of good health is increasingly equated with moral virtue: those who continue to 'choose' to smoke, drink or eat the wrong foods are irresponsible and deserving of their fate. This ignores the extent to which individual 'choices' for consumers are structured by powerful corporate interests in the brewing, food, tobacco and pharmaceutical industries. An effective preventive strategy which challenged these interests would seriously disrupt or impose great costs on capitalist producers.

Radical, feminist and Marxist approaches: a comment

Although a detailed critique of these three approaches is beyond the scope of the chapter, it may be helpful to highlight some of their strengths and weaknesses at this point.

The radical sociological critique of medicine provides important insights into the sources of professional power, and the way in which self-interest is rationalised in the public good even in the healing professions. The weaknesses are of exaggeration, and in Illich's case a romantic and utopian nostalgia for a past that never existed.

For example, by relying exclusively on mortality data the ineffectiveness of medical science is overstated. Its role in alleviating the pain and distress of non life-threatening illness is ignored. The account also exaggerates the extent to which the 'medicalisation of life' is a modern phenomenon. Strong (1979) argues that historical and anthropological evidence shows that life events like childbirth had long been medicalised, but with much worse outcomes for mothers and babies.

Similarly radicals overstate the degree of unanimity among the medical profession, which is in fact riven with dissension and competing ideologies. As Strong points out, the treatment of drug abuse, alcoholism and mental illness is marked by serious differences of opinion and some doctors have struggled to de-medicalise these areas in the face of the hostility of their peers.

Finally the sociological critique also exaggerates the credulity of the public about medicine's claims. Although some people may have an unhealthy reliance on doctors to relieve all the ills of this life, several studies show that most people are fairly sceptical about the efficacy of medical treatment and use many sources of advice and help, not just doctors and drugs (Calnan 1988; Blaxter 1983).

The radical attack from *within* medicine has proved to be more substantial and enduring. Cochrane's (1971) criticisms still seem as relevant and cogent today as they did 20 years ago, and at last seem to be taken seriously by the medical establishment and health policy-makers. Establishing the effectiveness and outcomes of health care in order to allocate resources more rationally has become a key policy issue in many countries.

The epidemiological critique has also strengthened. Re-evaluation of McKeown's data shows that if anything he *under-estimated* the role of the nineteenth century public health reforms in improving both mortality and morbidity (Sretzer 1988) and today public health medicine is starting to win the argument about how new health gains can be made.

Turning to feminist analyses, their strength lies in exposing the effects of gender relations and ideologies on women as producers and consumers of health care. They have succeeded in raising consciousness (and consciences) on many issues affecting women: the burdens of informal care, the effects of unsafe and unethical practices in contraception (particularly in the Third World), lack of choice and control in childbirth, the damaging effects of stereotyping in biasing doctors' diagnostic and treatment decisions for women patients.

But if issues like these have been put on the public agenda by feminists, the substantive gains they achieved were limited. Under successive Conservative administrations since 1979 traditional images of the family and the roles of women were reasserted. Sex equality slipped far down the political agenda and women had to fight hard to retain the rights they had won in the 1960s and 1970s on abortion, welfare benefits, maternity and employment rights. More significant than feminist campaigns in raising the profile of women in the NHS was the perception of a developing crisis in staff recruitment and retention, particularly in nursing, which is discussed in more detail in Chapter 3.

Finally, Marxist accounts appear to offer an impressively coherent and plausible explanation of the role of the capitalist state in health care, and the function of medicine in capitalist societies at the level of grand theory. But in spite of their strength in accounting for historical continuities and pulling together many diverse elements Marxist analyses cannot adequately account for the differences between capitalist health care systems and the details of their development, and the empirical evidence often contradicts the logic of the argument. For example the fact that 57 per cent of current spending on acute in-patients in the NHS is devoted to the 'unproductive' over-65s hardly supports the overall thesis. In the end, loading the whole weight of explanation onto the 'changing nature of capitalist interests' is tautological and actually explains very little.

In addition Marxist prescriptions ultimately depend on the revolutionary overthrow of capitalism by communism, an increasingly unlikely scenario when Marxism as both a political creed and movement has never been weaker. Instead the 1980s has seen neoliberal market philosophies being adopted even by parties of the Left. The retreat of Marxism has been paralleled by the ascendancy of the New Right.[2]

The New Right and the state

A substantial literature has emerged analysing the ideas of the New Right, the distinctions between different schools, and the reasons for their political and intellectual ascendancy in the 1980s. That discussion cannot be replicated here. It is sufficient to sketch in the broad outlines of the New Right critique of the interventionist state, and more specifically, the welfare state (drawing largely on Harris 1987; Clarke et al. 1987). Later chapters will try to disentangle in greater detail the effect of New Right ideas on actual Conservative health policies throughout the 1980s as one strand (albeit an important one) of influences in the skein of policy development.

The New Right attack was aimed at the social democratic consensus of the postwar years, a consensus which, as discussed earlier, was founded on the intellectual ascendancy of Fabian socialism underpinned by values of equality, equity, efficiency and social integration. The managed mixed economy and a highly developed system of collective social provision were the means for achieving these values.

Market liberal doctrines and policies were kept alive in these lean years by writers like Hayek and Friedman and right-wing policy institutes like the Institute of Economic Affairs and the Adam Smith Institute. These were tolerated as crankish anachronisms with negligible political influence.

But the economic and social prescriptions of Beveridge and Keynes seemed increasingly unable to reverse either economic decline or deal with the 'crisis of welfare' which in 1981 the Organisation for Economic Cooperation and Development (OECD) forecast for Western nations in the run-up to the next century. The supposed crisis resulted from rapidly growing numbers of elderly people in proportion to the number of wage earners in the population, low economic growth and taxpayer resentment at the 'burdens' of welfare. A yawning gap was forecast between anticipated social expenditures and resources. Particularly alarming were the estimated costs of pension commitments already undertaken, and the projected costs of stubbornly high continuing rates of unemployment (OECD 1981).

Keynesian economic management seemed unable to deal with the new phenomenon of stagflation – high inflation coupled with low growth and high unemployment – and market liberals mounted a strong attack on the welfare state as the cause of Britain's economic problems.

The core of the neoliberal argument is the need to free enterprise and initiative from the dead hand of the state. The ill-effects of state interference in the economy take several forms. First, state planning and regulation of the economy inhibit its efficient operation by distorting market forces. Second, the government taxes its citizens excessively to fund public expenditure, and excessive taxation blunts risk-taking and economic effort. Third, a large public sector aids economic decline since it does not create wealth whereas the private sector does.

The interventionist state has political as well as economic ill-effects by inducing unrealistic expectations on the part of voters and electoral trade-offs between parties bargaining for votes. This results in the 'overload' thesis. Excessive demands are placed on governments by sectional interest groups beyond their capacity to meet them. Repeated government 'failure' results not only in a withdrawal of support from specific administrations by the electorate but eventually disillusionment with the institutions and processes of political democracy itself.

These general arguments for 'rolling back the state' underpin a more specific critique of the state's role in welfare which revolves around two themes: economic efficiency and moral values. Regarding the first theme, it is claimed that the provision of welfare by state monopolies leads to waste since they are protected from the efficiency-inducing pressure of market competition. Comprehensive state welfare also induces dependency, reduces incentives to work, and blunts initiative and enterprise. Regarding the second theme, market liberals concur with radical liberals like Illich that professionals and bureaucrats tend to promote their own interests rather than meeting the needs of their clients. Hence far from state welfare being a morally superior form of meeting social needs, as claimed by Fabian socialists, for the New Right state welfare is paternalistic and morally bankrupt, rationing resources in a biased and potentially discriminatory way. Individuals are coerced in two ways: as taxpayers forced to pay for wasteful services and as consumers denied any choice over the level or type of services they wish to consume.

The New Right also deny the role of welfare in promoting social integration. Titmuss's concept of society as an organic entity is, for market liberals, simply metaphysics: society is no more than the individuals and families who make it up. Integration is achieved through the impersonal (and nondiscriminatory) mechanisms of the market. But families owe responsibilities to each other, and for humanitarian and religious reasons the duty of charity to others. State welfare, it is claimed, undermines both kinds of obligation.

The National Health Service as a public sector monopoly was an exemplar of everything the New Right most criticise. It appeared to have an irresistible momentum for growth demanded by its one million employees and supported by public opinion. The major resource users, doctors, were not held accountable for spending taxpayers' money. There were no fiscal incentives for the spenders to economise or for consumers to limit their demands. In addition to lack of choice the public tolerated standards of service which they would never dream of tolerating in the private sector.

The solutions offered by New Right commentators and their fate is the subject of later chapters. It is worth pointing out however that the neoliberal perspective concentrates on the efficient delivery and financing of services and on issues of consumer choice. There is no explicit critique of prevailing medical definitions of health and illness, and no vision about what the goals of health policy should be (since by definition consumer choice in the market determines priorities). In this respect it differs from the four perspectives discussed earlier in the chapter, which converge in adopting a social model of health for a restructuring of priorities and goals.

In contrast neoliberals' emphasis on individual choice and personal responsibility for health makes them underestimate the importance of environmental factors. Policy strategies which attack the social and economic determinants of ill-health are dismissed as futile attempts at social engineering.

Conclusions

This chapter has looked at the main academic and political perspectives which have shaped thinking on health and health care. Many of the themes and issues raised will re-emerge in later chapters. In terms of policy influence the New Right captured the intellectual and political high ground in Britain and many other countries throughout the 1980s. In the post-Thatcher era, and as both Labour and Conservative parties return to the centre ground, it is tempting to see those years as an aberration, tempting but false since the parameters of the debate have fundamentally shifted.

Notes

1. From a post-structuralist perspective, Foucault's (1973) account of the history of medicine shows how the development of hospitals from the end of the eighteenth century crucially affected these developments, framing both the organisation of medical ideas and the language in which they were embodied.
2. For an example of Marxist analysis used as a partial explanation for British health policies in the 1980s, see Harrison *et al.*, 1990.

References

Bevan, A. (1961) *In Place of Fear*, London: E P Publishing.

Blaxter, M. (1983) 'The causes of disease: women talking', *Social Science and Medicine* 17 (2): 59–69.

Brotherston, J. (1976) 'Inequality: is it inevitable?', in C. O. Carter and J. Peel (eds) *Equalities and Inequalities in Health*, London: Academic Press.

Calnan, M. (1988) 'Lay evaluation of medicine and medical practice: Report of a pilot study', *International Journal of Health Services* 18 (2) 311–22.

Clarke, J., Cochrane, A. and Smart, C. (1987) *Ideologies of Welfare: From Dreams to Disillusion,* London: Hutchinson Education.

Cochrane, A. (1971) *Effectiveness and Efficiency: Random Reflections on Health Services*, London: Nuffield Provincial Hospitals Trust.

Crosland, A. (1956) *The Future of Socialism*, London: Cape.

Department of Health and Social Security (1980) *Inequalities in Health* (The Black Report), London: HMSO.

Ehrenreich, J. (1978) *The Cultural Crisis of Modern Medicine*, New York: Monthly Review Press.

——and English, D. (1979) *For Her Own Good: 100 Years of the Experts' Advice to Women*, London: Pluto Press.

Forster D.P. (1976) 'Social class differences in sickness and general practitioner consultations', *Health Trends* 8: 29–32.

Foucault, M. (1973) *The Birth of the Clinic: an archaeology of perception*, London: Tavistock.

Freidson, (1970a) *Professional Dominance: The Social Structure of Medical Care*, New York: P Atherton.

——(1970b) *Profession of Medicine: A Study of the Sociology of Applied Knowledge*, New York: Harper Row.

Garnikov, E. (1978) 'Sexual division of labour: the case of nursing', in A. Kuhn and A. M. Wolpe (eds) *Feminism and Materialism*, London: Routledge.

George, V. and Wilding, P. (1976) *Ideology and Social Welfare*, London: Routledge and Kegan Paul.

Harris, D. (1987) *Justifying State Welfare*, Blackwell.

Harrison, S., Hunter, D. and Pollitt, C. (1990) *The Dynamics of British Health Policy*, London: Unwin Hyman.

Hart, T. (1971) 'The inverse care law', *Lancet* 1: 405–12.

Illich, I. (1976) *Limits to Medicine: Medical Nemesis*, 2nd edn, London: Marion Boyars.

Klein, R. (1989) *The Politics of the NHS*, 2nd edn, London: Longman.

Le Grand, J. (1982) *The Strategy of Equality: Redistribution and the Social Services*, London: Allen and Unwin.

McKeown, T. (1976) *The Modern Rise of Population and the Role of Medicine: Dream, Mirage or Nemesis?*, Rock Carling Monograph, London: Nuffield Provincial Hospitals Trust.

McKinlay, J. B. and Stoeckle, J. (1988) 'Corporatization and the social transformation of doctoring', *International Journal of Health Services* 18 (2): 191–203.

Navarro, V. (1986) *Crisis, Health and Medicine*, London: Tavistock.

Oakley, A. (1983) 'Women and health care', in J. Lewis (ed) *Women's Welfare, Women's Rights*, London: Croom Helm.

Organisation for Economic Cooperation and Development (1981) *The Welfare State in Crisis*, Paris: OECD.

Sretzer, S. (1988) 'The importance of social intervention in Britain's mortality decline 1850–1914: a reinterpretation of the role of public health', *Social History of Medicine* 1: 1–37.

Strong, P. M. (1979) 'Sociological imperialism and the profession of medicine', *Social Science and Medicine* 13a: 199–215.

Titmuss, R. (1963) *Essays on the Welfare State*, 2nd edn, London: Allen and Unwin.

CHAPTER 3

Scanning the future: the environmental context

'Change is not what it used to be' (Handy 1989).

The ideological debates which surround the NHS often seem to take place in a vacuum, oblivious to the massive social, economic and technological changes which are taking place in postindustrial societies. Like any other major social institution, the NHS will be profoundly affected by these developments.

This chapter looks at change in three major areas. Part 1 discusses the effects of economic restructuring, the debates surrounding 'post-Fordist' developments, and their significance for the delivery of welfare. Part 2 examines the questions posed by demographic change and how the NHS is affected, both as an employer and provider of services. Finally Part 3 examines some of the new dilemmas and opportunities posed by developments in medical technology and the related sciences and the need to subject these to ethical and economic scrutiny.

Part 1 – Facing up to the information age

Handy (1989) argues that while most people would accept that the pace of change has speeded up, few realise its scale and ferocity. Profound technological developments have already critically restructured the economies of developed societies from the production of things to the production of knowledge. The evidence lies in the changing occupational structure, in particular the shift away from manufacturing to service industry. Manufacturing employment fell in Britain by over one third from 1971 to 1990, to barely 23 per cent of all employees, with a corresponding one-third increase in the service sector. The main growth in the service sector, however, has been in jobs which are connected in some way with information. For example employment in banking, insurance and finance doubled from 1971–1990 (Dept. of Employment 1991).

The evidence is clearer from the United States, where the trends are even further developed. Naisbitt argues that employment in the traditional service sector (for example, catering, cleaning, distribution) has remained fairly stable since 1950 at around one-tenth of the labour force. But whereas only 17 per cent of employees worked in information jobs in 1950, by 1982 this had risen to 60 per cent compared to 13 per cent in manufacturing (Naisbitt 1984: 14).

It seems clear that some of the 'megatrends' of the information age will reverse those associated with industrial society. First, the falling real cost of information technology (IT) permits considerable decentralisation of production to take place, without loss of administrative control. These developments could open up new vistas of flexible working for large numbers of employees, who no longer need to be herded together in downtown locations for eight hours a day.

Second, the information society leads to a flattening of hierarchies. The control and communication functions of middle management become redundant when everyone has access to their own computer terminal. In addition the information society substitutes brain for brawn: 70 per cent of its jobs require intellectual skills and at least half of them require a professional qualification or education to degree standard. Such workers are expensive and in short supply, cannot be managed by the old 'command and control' hierarchies, and expect more scope for creativity and autonomy in their work. There is another reason why hierarchy will become obsolete. Information is by its nature a shared resource. Once produced it is hard to control, infinitely 'leaky'. If knowledge is power, then power is going to be dispersed.

Deeper explanations for the emergence of the information economy have centred around debates about the changing nature of capital accumulation in postindustrial societies, from 'Fordist' forms of mass production and standardised consumption patterns, to 'post-Fordist' forms of more flexible production to meet a growing diversity of consumer tastes. Although a detailed examination of the thesis is beyond the scope of the chapter (see, for instance, Sayer 1989), some of the trends which underpin the debate will be outlined, drawing on a major survey of companies by the Henley Centre for Forecasting (1991).

First, competition became fiercer in the 1980s with the deregulation of many markets both nationally and internationally, and the entry of new competitors (from the sunrise economies of the Far East for example). Second, the pace of technological development meant that the advantages to companies from new products or improvements were short-lived and soon overtaken by others. Third, markets also became increasingly fragmented as rising affluence led to increasing demands for differentiated products from discriminating purchasers. Markets become more complex when not only price, quality and image affect the purchasing decision but other considerations such as the environmental compatibility of products do as well.

Companies have sought to deal with these pressures in ways which reduce their fixed overheads, increase their responsiveness to their markets and enhance their capacity to adapt and deal with change.

Flexibility and decentralisation have become the new key words. Many companies have considerably slimmed down and changed their corporate structures. Much more autonomy is given to subsidiary companies although they must still meet key financial and policy targets. IT provides the 'organisational glue' for corporate objectives to be maintained within looser federal structures of inter dependent companies.

Internal structures modelled on the 'organismic' organisation, (Burns and Stalker 1961) with flexible project-based teams, are better placed to respond rapidly to change than fixed hierarchies. IT also allows greater devolution of decision-making to the lowest practical level and allows operational staff to take responsibility for ever-widening aspects of their total work: accessing information, planning, budgeting, delivery and quality control. In theory this should make the content of jobs more satisfying and skilled, and allow more scope for innovation. 'Flexibility' is also enhanced by contracting out peripheral or noncore functions. Handy argues that an efficient organisational design for the future is the 'shamrock' organisation: one leaf of the shamrock contains the 'core' professional staff, those with the crucial knowledge on which the organisation depends, from whom much is expected and to whom much is given. The expense of this 'core' group forces organisations to shed all noncore activities and staff to specialist contractors who in theory do the work better and at less cost. This is the second leaf of the shamrock.

Finally there is the flexible workforce of part-timers and temporary workers which has seen the biggest employment growth since the early 1980s, particularly in the service sector, and accounts for the majority of the growth in female employment. By this means the organisation tries to adapt to peaks and troughs in demand without taking on the burden of high fixed labour costs. The workforce therefore becomes increasingly polarised and fragmented, between the skilled and unskilled, core and periphery, and between the knowledge workers and those who lack the qualifications to join their ranks.

'Post-Fordism' and the Welfare State

Some analysts (for example, Hoggett 1987) have assumed an almost automatic convergence between post-Fordist developments in production and similar developments in welfare, public administration and politics.

Decentralisation of government, greater consumer choice in the welfare sector, a larger informal or voluntary welfare sector and more spontaneous or networked forms of political organisation are all supposed to follow . . .

(Rustin 1989: 58)

The causal links however are by no means clear. To some extent these changes may be consumer driven, reflecting consumer dissatisfaction with impersonal and bureaucratised welfare systems in contrast with the range of choice in private markets. In part they are driven by the need to effect productivity improvements in the public sector, and IT once more becomes the means to achieve this. However Rustin argues that the developments that have taken place in the public sector owe much more to conscious political choice: 'Thatcherism may be understood as a strategy of post-Fordism from the perspectives of the right' (Rustin 1989: 75). Policies of 'hiving-off' non core services, compulsory competitive tendering in local government and the health service, a greater role for the private and voluntary sectors in the provision of welfare and the more effective incorporation of business into the 'local state' (Cochrane 1991) have all been politically willed, often against considerable opposition.

Cochrane argues that it is difficult to see whether the direction of change can be described as 'post-Fordist' at all since the changes incorporate contradictory tendencies. For example, to enable inhouse teams to win catering and cleaning contracts in local authorities and the health service, labour has had to submit to more rigid disciplines and hierarchical control, not less. Similarly contracting-out may not provide authorities with greater flexibility if they are tied to long-term arrangements which are difficult to renegotiate.

Since a Conservative government has been elected for a fourth term these developments will probably continue. Even if the Labour party had won, it is difficult to say how far the developments were reversible. For example the Labour party planned to abolish compulsory competitive tendering in the public sector although many managers would have still continued with the practice if convinced it brought efficiency gains. Proposals on the minimum wage and protection of workers' rights (through endorsement of the EC's Social Chapter for example) if implemented might have helped prevent exploitation of the 'peripheral' workforce although the market advantage of the knowledge workers would continue.

With regard to the welfare sector, four developments are worth highlighting. First, the use of IT is growing rapidly and potentially has great scope in improving the technical efficiency of services and more personalised forms of delivery. For example the NHS has nearly completed the computerization of specific functions such as finance, patient administration systems in GP surgeries and acute hospitals, personnel, and so on. Coverage for medical audit, nurse management and case mix within acute hospitals should be completed by 1995 (NHSME 1991). Thereafter the real gains lie in integrating systems and electronic data sharing between organisations to improve the coordination of patient care across primary, secondary and community settings.

Second, at the end of the Thatcher years welfare services have become more fragmented and pluralistic, characterised by 'a blurring of boundaries and diffusion of power' (Klein 1987) as the private and voluntary sectors take on new and more important roles as providers, and new types of public–private partnerships are formed. This has important implications for the style and skills required by public managers (discussed in Chapter 6).

Third, the polarisation between information workers and the rest could take particularly sharp form in the welfare services which employ large numbers of semiskilled workers as carers and in the ancillary services. It will be an important challenge in future to imbue their work with dignity, self-esteem and value.

Finally, and on an optimistic note, if information technology is used to structure the organisation of work in ways which allow more people greater flexibility and choice it becomes possible to share different kinds of work more equitably. At present, as feminists point out, two-thirds of women do two jobs: paid in the labour market and unpaid at home. The result is not choice but the double shift. Home and childrearing commitments dictate the terms and conditions on which women can work so that overwhelmingly at present they are forced into the third leaf of the shamrock as low-paid semiskilled part-timers. Once again this is particularly notable in the health service, in which 70 per cent of employees are female.

Nevertheless it seems that part-time work is popular. Two-thirds of part-time workers surveyed in 1990 did not want a full-time job (Dept. of Employment 1991). If given a choice many workers of both sexes in the 'core' leaf of the shamrock would prefer a better balance between time and money and this could bring enormous advantages: greater sharing of child care between the sexes (which many men now want), more opportunities to study or retrain in later life and the possibility of wider participation in public affairs or voluntary work.

Part 2 – Facing up to demography

Much has been written about the ageing of Western populations and its economic consequences but few realise the extent of demographic change and its full implications into the twenty-first century. The facts for this country are as follows.

Declining fertility
Britain faced a 35 per cent reduction in the number of 18-year-olds in the decade 1984–1994 with most of the reduction taking place after 1990. This marks a long-term trend of declining fertility which appears to have stabilised at 1.8 births per woman, below population replacement rate.

An ageing workforce
The number of people in the working age group (16–65) was 32

million in 1985, of whom 26 million were economically active (Thompson 1987) The age group will grow marginally till the end of the century but due to the precipitate drop in the younger age groups a sustained period of ageing within the working population has begun.

More women working

Nearly 90 per cent of the overall increase in the labour force of 3.1 million between 1971 and 1990 was accounted for by the increased participation of women. This trend will continue, with women taking most of the one million jobs projected for the 1990s. By the end of the century women will make up 45 per cent of the total civilian labour force. This will reinforce the trend to lower fertility. Once women can control unexpected births through contraception they spend longer in the labour force and invest more in education and qualifications which in turn increases their earning potential and makes the economic incentives against starting a family more marked. This is borne out by research on birth rates since 1952: higher earnings for women depress the birth rate, higher earnings for men raise it (Ermisch 1990). Additionally Britain's high divorce rate (37 per cent in 1991) and the economic insecurity experienced by lone mothers is another incentive for women to stay in the workforce and increase their skills.

Growing numbers of elderly people

The number of people over 60 will be relatively stable till the end of the century, but within the total group those over 80 rise rapidly from 1.8 million in 1985 to 2.6 million by 2011 (Thompson 1987). As a proportion of the total age group of 60+ those over 75 will have risen from 38.2 to 47.2 per cent during the years 1989–2001. The health and social service needs of the elderly rise exponentially with age. Annual health spending (hospital and community health services only) on a 65–74 year old in 1988 averaged £1087, and for someone over 85 £1995, compared to £85 for a person aged 16–64 (Robinson 1991).

Demographic trends and the labour market: the pitfalls of prediction

The implications of demographic trends for problems of labour supply received considerable coverage in the last few years, with analysts predicting fierce competition for new entrants to the labour market and serious shortages of skilled and educated staff. A report from the Institute of Manpower Studies in 1987 forecast rising demand for managers (up 12 per cent between 1987–1995), scientific and engineering professionals (up 21 per cent) and other professionals (up 17 per cent) (IMS 1987). Occupations such as these were expected to account for three-quarters of the net job growth in this period, and employers were advised to look beyond their traditional 'preferred' groups when recruiting. Even in 1990 when the recession had started to bite deeply 46 per cent of employers in a major survey carried out by the Training Agency reported recruiting difficulties (*Guardian* 14 September 1990).

As the main public sector recruiter of qualified staff, the NHS faced particular difficulties. In the survey mentioned above, the health sector was second only to mechanical engineering in the proportion of employers experiencing difficulties. Many of the skills the NHS needs are easily transferable and salaries are not competitive with the private sector, for example accountants, information specialists, laboratory technicians and secretaries.

But most concern was expressed about nursing, which comprises 50 per cent of the total NHS workforce. To replenish the nursing stock the NHS had become the biggest public sector recruiter of qualified labour, taking one in three of female school leavers with between five 'O' levels or GCSEs and two 'A' levels. Some of the more alarmist projections estimated this would need to rise to one in two in the early 1990s to maintain current intake patterns (Callender and Pearson 1989). There was a clear need for action.

Who will care? A case study of nursing

The NHS has traditionally recruited large numbers of learners to compensate for high wastage rates from the profession. These were particularly marked during training, with only about 65 per cent of an initial intake completing their course and registering (Hutt 1989). Thereafter about 10 per cent of qualified staff left annually, particularly in the younger age groups which is partially compensated for by the re-entry of qualified staff.

National 'net' wastage figures have been declining in recent years so that although learner intakes have declined from 30,000 to 18,000 between 1981–87, the total qualified workforce increased from 212,000 to 239,000 (Grocott 1989). Nevertheless high wastage of student learners and the instability of the nursing workforce combined with projections of an increasingly competitive labour market to force major changes on the profession and its recruitment and retention strategies. There are three main aspects to the changes, which are all interrelated.

First, there has been a harder look at the components of the nursing process to assess whether nursing skills were appropriately used and related to the needs of patients or whether they followed old-established but unvalidated local custom and practice. Several recent investigations (Beardshaw and Davies 1990, DHSS 1986, Mersey RHA 1989) concluded that trained and student staff are often used wastefully on tasks better performed by support staff or to cover deficiencies in paramedical cover. More fundamentally, Beardshaw and Davies argue that the demarcation lines between medical, nursing and other types of health worker require comprehensive reappraisal.

Traditional assumptions about professional boundaries and working practices will have to be challenged to bring about a more cost-effective deployment of trained staff.

Secondly, the education and training of nurses and associated workers is being radically restructured in line with the Project 2000 proposals of the United Kingdom Central Council for Nursing, Midwifery and Health Visiting (UKCC), published in 1986. Project 2000 argued the necessity for change as much in terms of keeping pace with service needs and professional nursing developments as tackling the deficiencies of existing nurse training and the challenges posed to recruitment by demographic trends.

The main proposal was the creation of a single level of registered nurse through a three year training programme. Enrolled training would be phased out as fast as possible, with existing enrolled nurses given opportunities for conversion courses. Student nurses should be supernumary for their whole training, not used as exploited 'pairs of hands' on the wards, one of the worst aspects of traditional training patterns. All student nurses would study a common two-year foundation programme with specialisms developing after that. The authors expected more specialist practitioners to develop in all aspects of hospital and community nursing, acting as team leaders in many cases. The 'new nurse' would have a higher and broader level of competencies, expected to make and be fully accountable for all decisions regarding the care given to patients.

Complementing the role of the 'new nurse' is the new health care assistant. The role has evolved as a basic but flexible care worker, with a minimum of three months skill-based training. At the first level training will be primarily on-the-job but assistants can secure a vocational qualification obtained over two years validated by the National Council for Vocational Qualifications. This will be a flexible qualification which can be used in other sectors of the caring industry, or be traded up to enable access to nursing, social work or other occupations. Through this system of flexible 'bridges and ladders' the NHS hoped to tap new sources of labour into nursing itself, from unqualified school leavers, previously unemployed middle-aged women and men.

The final plank of the strategy is designed to improve the attractiveness of nursing as a career in competition with others. To begin with the nursing career structure was regraded into nine main clinical grades in 1988, in line with qualifications and the responsibilities of the job. This was matched by substantial pay rises, particularly for more senior grades, and bursaries for Project 2000 student learners.

Recognising, seemingly for the first time, the needs of their overwhelmingly female labour force, health authorities introduced equal opportunity policies and started to experiment with crèches, job sharing, flexible working, stay-in-touch schemes for staff taking career breaks and much more besides.

However the predicted shortage of qualified nursing staff not only failed to materialise, but many newly qualified nurses are unable to find employment. The extraordinary depth and length of the recession is partly to blame, since one effect has been to reduce wastage rates still further. But moves by managers to 'rationalise' skillmix, substituting unqualified for qualified staff, are even more important. Between September 1990 and 1991 the NHS lost 15,400 qualified nurses – a drop of 5.2 per cent – but the number of unqualified staff rose by 137,400, a rise of 17 per cent. This changed the ratio of qualified to unqualified staff from 61:23 to 58:28. Furthermore the new clinical grading structure makes skillmix exercises easier to undertake, since the responsibilities expected from each grade of nurse are precisely spelt out.[1] Instead of expanding nurse training, colleges are planning a substantial reduction in intakes.

As the anticipated 'crisis' fades from memory, we might also expect managers to show less concern for improving the career prospects and conditions of work of nurses. However, the enthusiastic way in which the present Health Secretary, Virginia Bottomley, has implemented Opportunity 2000 in the NHS (the government's equal opportunity initiative for women) and set clear targets for health authorities to achieve, should ensure that momentum is not entirely lost.

The case study illustrates that the implications of demographic trends can be modified by unforeseen economic events but they can also be successfully addressed by policy planning. Taken together the three strands of the nursing 'package' represented a major attempt to meet future demographic challenges. The 'crisis' was also used as an opportunity to bring the education and training of nurses in line with the demands of the twenty-first century, acknowledging some of the trends discussed earlier in the chapter. For example there is explicit acknowledgement of the trends towards decentralised work patterns. Increasingly nurses and their assistants will work in many different health care settings in the community, often in multidisciplinary teams, aided by information technology to relay essential information for planning and resource management purposes to small 'head office' staffs. Already many district nurses and health visitors record details of their work on hand held terminals, rather than in written notes.

The split between 'knowledge workers' and the rest is prefigured in the highly trained professional nurses (whom Project 2000 authors call 'knowledgeable doer[s]'), expensive and therefore fewer in number, and the health care assistants who do most of the basic physical tasks of care. There is also through the training strategy an attempt to give this work greater dignity and esteem.

In conclusion, the remodelling of nursing is a good example of attempts both to modernise the profession and address future problems of labour supply posed by an ageing population. Whether it can also address the issues of caring for growing numbers of elderly people is another matter. This is another aspect of demographic change which has attracted considerable attention and triggered alarmist projections about the burdens and costs of care. However these projections may be based on assumptions which also require re-examination.

Demographic change and the costs of care

Growth in the number of elderly people in the population is one important source of growing demands on health services. People over 65 consume over 45 per cent of total health spending. But policy assumptions about the economic costs of the elderly in future are premissed on bleak models of ageing and the ageing process, which Gail Wilson summarises as 'downhill all the way' (Wilson 1991).

Western attitudes to old people have historically been negative, portraying the 'seventh age of man' as one of helplessness and decline. Policy statements on the elderly have similarly reflected the view that old age is associated with an irreversible decline into disability and dependency regardless of differences in income, class, gender and race which significantly affect the experience of ageing. Means (1988) argues that some authors treat the total group of 'pensioners' (a group which may cover 40 years given the trend to early retirement) as a 'special needs' category.

Bleak scenarios of the 'economic burden' that elderly people imposed on the working population underlay the 1988 Social Security Act and the impetus given to private pensions. It also drove the response of early Thatcher governments to health and social care for the elderly. For example the Health Advisory Service (1983) warned of a 'rising tide' of senile dementia which could 'overwhelm the entire health care system' and a consultative paper in 1981 argued that the informal, voluntary and private sectors must play a bigger role in the provision of care.

There is however a growing body of work which challenges the models of ageing which underpin current policies. Walker (1980, 1987), Townsend (1981) and Bosanquet (1987) have argued that old people are forced into dependency by the rest of society through early retirement policies, stigmatising social security, and welfare services which undermine independence.

The view that growing numbers of elderly people inevitably mean a growing and costly burden of disability in future has also been challenged. As a growing proportion of the population escapes premature mortality to live out their natural life span, Fries (1989) argues that this need not mean adding infirm years to life. There is now considerable scope for pushing back the onset of morbidity in old age into fewer and fewer years with properly targeted health promotion and illness prevention policies and the widespread adoption of healthier lifestyles. With this 'terminal drop' model of ageing (Wilson 1991) old people stay reasonably healthy and independent till some final trauma takes them off.

Health promotion strategies aimed at elderly people could be a highly cost-effective option for the NHS as Fries's research trial with 6,000 retirees in California demonstrates (reported in Maynard 1990). The sample, all holders of Blue Cross medical insurance policies, were divided into three. One group received a low-cost health promotion package, a second only received questionnaires and the control group was monitored through their medical insurance claims. By the end of 12 months the first group recorded 20 per cent lower medical claims than the other two, and the savings amounted to six times the cost of the health promotion package they had received.

Nevertheless for the foreseeable future a considerable proportion of elderly people will require care at specific periods of their lives. For example those over 75 are six times more likely to receive a home help than those aged 64–75. The proportion of those over 85 unable to bathe, shower or wash all over is seven times higher than those in the 65–69 age group (Walker 1987).

Acknowledging the extent of social need in the elderly does not mean accepting that dependency irreversibly deepens with age, from mild to intense. Wilson (1991) argues that in reality most old people can live well and independently with properly targeted inputs of help at times of crisis or illness. In other words people move in and out of dependent states (just as younger people do) and the help they receive can either enforce dependency permanently or provide the temporary support they need to recover. For example, many old people living alone have been forced to move into residential care when experiencing a temporary crisis (perhaps a broken hip or a mild stroke) in the absence of suitable emergency domiciliary care.

A growing recognition that services should be adapted to the needs of individual users to sustain independence underlies present community care policies, set out in the White Paper 'Caring for People' (DOH 1989). The philosophy marks a welcome shift from earlier Conservative policy. However the slow pace of implementation and the problems experienced by local authorities in planning, managing and funding community care means that in practice many family carers will see little change or increased help for a long time.

The bulk of care for elderly people takes place within family settings. The most comprehensive national picture of informal carers undertaken by the General Household Survey 1985 shows that 3.5 million women and 2.5 million men had caring responsibilities, though this is disproportionately the care of an elderly spouse for men. In the 45–64 age group one quarter of women are carers compared to 16 per cent of men (Green 1988).

Even if issues of social justice are ignored, the demographic evidence demonstrates the folly of relying so heavily on middle-aged women as informal carers. First, the available pool is shrinking. This is due to several factors. Families are growing smaller and greater geographical mobility means that relatives are less likely to be close at hand in times of need. The trend for women to enter and stay in the labour market is probably irreversible. The extent of family break-up means that divorced women must work to support themselves and their children (90 per cent of lone parents are women). Added to the problem of divorce is the fact that 34 per cent of marriages now involve the remarriage of one or more partners. This can lead to confused feelings of obligation towards ex-parents-in-law, stepgrandmothers, and so on. How many women would be able or willing to care for distant relatives by marriage?

Caring for People

Six main objectives

1 Services which allow people to remain in their own homes whenever possible.
2 High priority to supporting carers.
3 Quality care to be based on needs assessment and good case management.
4 To promote a 'mixed economy' of welfare.
5 To clarify responsibilities.
6 Better value for money.

Main features

1 Local authority as the lead agency: Local authority social service departments are given lead responsibility for community care. Their role will include:
   - assessing individual need (in collaboration with health authority staff);
   - appointing case managers to design individually tailored packages of care;
   - providing services and purchasing them from other providers;
   - monitoring quality and cost-effectiveness;
   - assessing clients' ability to help pay for the care they receive.

2 Developing a mixed economy of care: Local authorities will be expected to use a variety of voluntary and private providers as well as their own services, making more use of competitive tendering for care contracts to secure value for money.

3 Planning and collaboration: Local authorities to publish community care plans for approval by April 1991 in consultation with health, housing and family health service authorities.
   Joint planning with health authorities to be based on 'planning agreements' which set out common goals for community care, funding arrangements, agreed operational policies in key areas, and so on.

---

4 Quality control: Local authorities to set up 'arms-length' inspection units to monitor the quality of all public and private residential homes according to uniform standards.

5 Resources: Interim specific grant to be paid by RHAs to local authorities from 1991–92 to set up priority community care projects for people with mental illness.

   New unified budget to cover the cost of social care whether this is in the person's own home or in a residential care or nursing home. The new budget to be paid to local authorities will include the care element of social security payments to people in private and voluntary homes. The rights of those already in homes will be protected but in future local authorities will determine whether residential care is appropriate to the person's needs and what proportion of the costs should be met from public funds. These arrangements were to begin from April 1991, but have been delayed to April 1993.

   The government decided to 'ring fence' the community care budget when the first allocation was announced in November 1992, and not make it part of the general grant to local authorities as announced in the White Paper.

The 'pool' of carers is also growing older. As more people live to ages of 85 plus, the age of their carers also increases and elderly carers will be less able to cope. One of the saddest aspects of this issue is the heavy strains and burdens placed on elderly people who might have expected their last years to be more enjoyable.

In conclusion the challenges posed by an ageing population need radical rethinking and immense cultural changes in attitudes. The resources, powers and energies of older people need to be positively harnessed and policies should be geared to sustaining their independence for as long as possible. The growing consumer power of older people and the fact that already one in four voters is retired may help to bring this about. From the perspective of the NHS, considerable health gains and reductions in expenditure over the longer term could be achieved by expanding health promotion work with older people, a previously neglected group. More immediately, community care policies must be implemented with much greater vigour and political backing if Britain is not to face a 'crisis of caring' in the twenty-first century.

Part 3 – Pushing back the boundaries: developments in medical technology

If demography acts as a constraining context on health care provision, future developments in medical technology open up a bewildering scenario of choice. But medical advance not only enhances clinical capability, it carries with it profound ethical, legal, social and economic implications. Recent developments in the sale of organs for transplants, life support for profoundly handicapped or brain damaged patients, or the treatment of infertility have rehearsed some of the dilemmas and controversies. These will multiply in future with the development of new technologies and new branches of science such as molecular biology. This has developed rapidly since James Watson and Francis Crick broke the genetic code in 1962 by uncovering the structure of DNA and has opened up not only abstract genetic knowledge but the manipulation of genes and the basis of life itself.

One contentious area where ethical controversies abound concerns genetic screening and the detection of high risk groups. About three thousand inherited abnormalities, ranging from the serious to the mild, have already been identified by scientists and genome research continues to identify more. The pitfalls and dangers that knowledge brings with it are becoming apparent. For example, what is the value of screening for diseases for which there is no known cure such as Huntingdon's disease when that knowledge can destroy the future quality of life of individual carriers, as they await its possible onset? What suffering and distress are caused by the identification of 'false positives'? What controls should exist for using genetic knowledge in insurance and employment? Some genetic disorders predispose individuals to the toxic effects of substances found in the workplace or environment. Will employers be tempted to screen potential employees to protect themselves from lawsuits afterwards from workers who contract such diseases? Insurers might be similarly tempted to screen out high risks who may file earlier or more frequent claims due to illness or early death.

The progress of molecular biology (and its application, biotechnology) is pushing medicine into a new age, from the pharmacologic to the molecular. 'Gene splicing' already allows doctors to transplant 'healthy' genes into individuals suffering from inherited diseases, which raises ethical issues about the transplantation of animal or fetal tissue, but does not affect the future genetic stock. In the near future however scientists will be able to graft new genes into human eggs and embryos. This would have long-term genetic implications (*Independent* 21.8.90). At present about 10 per cent of pregnancies in Britain are at risk of producing a genetically 'diseased' baby. About 14,000 such babies are born annually of which half have serious conditions resulting in painful lives or early deaths. The issues surrounding genetic engineering of this sort are even more profound. Where does the search for 'perfection' stop? A development which starts from the humane desire to prevent severe handicap could lead to demands by parents for genetic interventions to produce traits which are thought to be culturally desirable, such as maleness and fair skin.

Turning to other developments, improvements in medical

technologies in current use signify a trend to safer, non-invasive and more efficient procedures, enabling shorter in-patient stays, more day case and outpatient treatment. Lasers have transformed specialities like ophthalmology and cardiac surgery and are set to transform even dentistry, replacing the dentist's drill within five years (*Independent* 19.3.92). Lithotripsy, which blasts kidney stones to gravel, shortens in-patient stays by 75 per cent compared to treatment by surgery and allows the patient to resume normal activities in 24 hours.

Imaging techniques continue to improve the safety and accuracy of diagnosis as magnetic resonance imaging and positron emission tomography are added to computerised tomography (CT scanners). Catheters and endoscopes can be used for safer and less painful investigations. Developments in biotechnology, in particular monoclonal antibodies, have made possible over-the-counter pregnancy and ovulation testing, and in future will enable many more diagnostic tests to be carried out simply in GP surgeries and the patient's home.

Technologies designed to replace or substitute for lost functions will also continue to improve, allowing if not complete recovery at least a greatly improved quality of life for patients. Stiller claims that almost any vital organ can now be transplanted, with 75 to 90 per cent of recipients achieving better health. 60 to 80 per cent of patients receiving a kidney, heart or liver transplant are fully rehabilitated and able to work (Stiller 1989). The prospect of artificial hearts replacing reliance on cadaver hearts is already in sight. A variety of improved 'implantable' devices like the newer types of pacemakers allow sensitive monitoring of essential functions to take place and adjustments to be made without further surgery. More sophisticated computer-designed prostheses for joint replacements allow many more patients to benefit.

One clear implication of many current advances is growing decentralisation of health care. Much more can be done out of hospital and in the GP's surgery, the patient's home or in low-technology settings. For example the growth of diagnostic kits mentioned earlier and the development of computerised 'expert systems' for diagnosis and selection of the most appropriate treatment can be used by the GP. New imaging and scanning equipment can transmit images away from the site of the machine since they use computers not X-ray film, allowing doctors at outlying sites to have recourse to specialist opinion relayed from a distance.

A further example relates to day case surgery. Patients still need to recuperate but do not need to stay in an acute hospital to do so. Experiments with 'patient hotels' or intensive nursing aftercare through 'hospitals at home' schemes have proved popular, high quality and less costly (Stocking 1991).

This brief survey of medical developments demonstrates that once again information technology is at the heart of them, both in terms of diagnostic and therapeutic techniques and in linking patient data across hospital, community and primary care settings. This in turn underpins the move to decentralised care and the stripping away of much that is done in acute hospitals today.

Evaluating medical technologies: dilemmas of choice

Sometimes new health care technologies produce savings on the ones they replace or allow more cost-effective patterns of care. Often they promise improvements at much greater cost, widening the gap between the possible and the affordable. Hence criteria to regulate and deploy their use become increasingly urgent. Up to 50 per cent of the rise in health spending in the United States has been attributed not only to the introduction of new technologies but to the inappropriate overuse of existing ones (Banta and Thacker 1990). Britain traditionally has a more cautious approach and the Department of Health (DOH) has greater control over the diffusion of high cost technologies through the system of designated regional and supra-regional specialities. But there appear to be few clear criteria governing the selection of these specialities and those which are experimental are not monitored or evaluated in any rigorous way (Hogg 1988). In addition to designated specialities which receive special funding, individual consultants may develop new techniques in district general hospitals which act as 'hidden' specialities, pulling funds away from other services.

As discussed in Chapter 2, it is precisely this 'misappropriation' of resources which draws the sharpest attacks from medicine's critics who would divert more resources into the 'low technology' care of the elderly and handicapped and effective illness prevention strategies. Lay opinion is ambivalent. Media publicity on the high technology marvels of medicine fuel exaggerated expectations of what new 'breakthroughs' can achieve. Expensive technology like CT scanners can attract charitable funding on a large scale. In addition the public reacts strongly to media 'scandals' of patients denied access to treatments like renal dialysis. But many people are also aware from personal experience that high technology medicine is used inappropriately and ineffectively, prolonging or inflicting unnecessary suffering.

Jennett's (1986) admirably dispassionate analysis of the issues throws much needed light into this confused debate. He points out that technological development in health care is a continuous process, and today's 'high tech' is tomorrow's 'low tech'. In addition the costs and benefits of new procedures change over time as they become diffused more widely and in comparison to available alternatives. New technology may represent a cost saving on older forms of treatment but still represents a cost push in overall terms by extending the boundaries of those who could potentially benefit.

Arguments on the pros and cons of high technology medicine are bedevilled by many false assumptions. One of these concerns the dichotomy between 'cure' versus 'care'. In practice much hospital medicine is neither. Jennett argues that 'most patients who now reach hospitals have progressive disease, the ultimate outcome of which cannot be influenced' (Jennett 1986: 4). This may be life-threatening like cancer, or nonlife-threatening but disabling like arthritis. Much high technology medicine is therefore palliative, alleviating the effects of the disease by relieving pain or restoring mobility. It is part of the panoply of measures available to the clinician in the total care and management of the patient, perhaps over many years.

Another false assumption is that diagnosis leads to therapy and therapy to cure. Campaigns for diagnostic technology like CT whole body scanners are often premised on the assumption that earlier diagnosis will lead to an improved outcome for patients. The evidence to substantiate this is limited to very few conditions. More often diagnosis reveals untreatable disease or leads to misplaced attempts at therapy. Jennett argues:

Much of the debate about therapeutic technology is about its failures. These result largely from its use in patients who either do not benefit at all or who derive only temporary improvement or whose rescue leaves them more severely disabled than they were.

(Jennett 1986: 13)

Much intensive care and cancer treatment falls into this category. The key message emerging from the discussion is that the deployment of medical technology, be it drugs, equipment or new procedures, must rest on rigorous and continuous assessments of effectiveness cost and safety, and the appropriate selection of patients who can benefit.

The outcomes movement

As the evidence for the misuse or overuse of health care technologies accumulates, most Western governments have responded by more formal systems of technology assessment and growing interest in what has been termed the 'outcomes movement' (Epstein 1990). The 'gold standard' for assessing clinical efficacy and safety is the randomised control trial (RCT), where the outcomes of alternative forms of treatment are compared experimentally. The results relate to well-controlled, essentially ideal conditions but may reveal little about the effectiveness or safety of a procedure in widespread use in ordinary clinical practice. Increasingly the availability of large computerised data bases offers the potential of supplementing RCTs with nonrandomised studies of tremendous size. The United States has led the way in collecting such data, necessary for government and private insurers setting reimbursement rates and paying bills to providers. However the data also allows the treatment patterns of hundreds of thousands of patients to be analysed and the outcomes of treatment to be monitored. 'Outcomes' were initially defined in limited terms to include mortality, complication and readmission rates. Recently however the outcomes considered valid indicators of health have been broadened to include such quality of life measures as emotional health, social interaction, functional status, degree of disability and so on. Increased emphasis is being placed on obtaining the views of patients themselves.

How should outcome data be used? There are three levels of application, each level impinging more strongly on clinical autonomy and patient choice.

1 Informing the decisions of clinicians and patients by providing information on the probabilities of success and risks associated with different treatment options. This requires disseminating information and educating clinicians to make use of it.
2 Establishing clinical guidelines and protocols such as those developed to aid purchasers by the DOH for the prevention, treatment and management of diseases such as cardiovascular disease or diabetes mellitus. Although advisory at present such protocols could be used to regulate clinician behaviour. In the United States, for example, insurers like Blue Cross have worked with medical societies to agree procedures and tests no longer justifiable in routine medical practice, which they will no longer reimburse.
3 Prioritising and rationing health care according to comparative assessments of cost and benefit.

The third approach is most contentious. Its best known proponent in Britain is Alan Maynard who developed the QALY or quality-adjusted life year. QALYs are a method of assessing the health benefits of a given procedure against the resources used to achieve it. Hence the cost of achieving one QALY for renal dialysis might be equal to 19 hip replacements or 190 preventive advice sessions on smoking by GPs. Benefits are defined as improvements in life expectancy adjusted for changes in four key indicators of quality of life: physical mobility, capacity for self-care, freedom from pain and distress and social adjustment. If life expectancy improves when all four indicators are held constant or also improve then clearly an unambiguous benefit to health has taken place. The value of extra years of life diminishes however if one or more of these quality factors declines or cannot be assured. Hence the need for quality-adjusted life years.

A bold experiment to use outcome data to determine priorities for state funding of health care has been tried by the state of Oregon in the United States. In America, health care is largely private, with only the Medicaid and Medicare programmes providing a safety net for the poor and elderly. The federal government pays 63 per cent of the cost of Medicaid, leaving the states to find the rest of the money. Oregon only provided Medicaid to those whose incomes were 58 per cent below the federal poverty line. In 1989 however they decided to bring more people into Medicaid up to 100 per cent of the line, by restricting the number of treatments it would pay for.

A Health Care Commission was set up to rank hundreds of treatments in order of priority, using a formula similar to QALYs. The Commission also undertook extensive public research through community meetings and telephone surveys. The public were asked to specify the values they thought should underpin funding decisions and what, in general terms, their priorities were, and this too was fed into the data base. The state legislature decided the overall budget and this was used to determine the cut-off point, below which treatments ranked low priority would not be funded. This included transplant surgery and medical treatment for AIDS (but not 'comfort care' for those in the last stages of the illness).

The criticism the Oregon experiment has received highlights the general difficulties of moving towards this kind of explicit rationing system. For example:

1   What is a socially just basis for valuing states of health? Is the restoration of health to be valued more highly in the young than the old, the productive than the nonproductive or have all lives equal value?
2   Whose values count? Although the Oregon Health Commission made strenuous efforts to involve the public, two-thirds of those attending the meetings were graduate educated professionals, and 60 per cent of those were health care workers. The poor and sick were poorly represented.
3   What is the quality of information on 'benefit' which goes into the exercise? Doctors rarely agree on the 'best' form of treatment but their opinions are not based on good clinical evaluative research since 70 per cent of treatments are still unvalidated.
4   What is the ethical justification of barring access to treatments which *some* individuals may benefit from?

The Oregon combination of technical expert opinion and public participation was at first seized on with enthusiasm by many NHS managers as a means of legitimising rationing decisions. But the difficulties experienced by Oregon have demonstrated that there is no technical fix. Increasingly the Oregon Commissioners have had to abandon cost-benefit or cost-effectiveness criteria because of inadequacies of data. Claims to scientific rationality, which were always dubious, have given way to the increasing use of value judgements (Klein 1992). (The methodology underpinning QALYs has also been heavily criticised, see Mulkay *et al.*, 1987; Loomes and McKenzie 1989; Carr-Hill 1988a, 1988b.)

However the explosion of medical advance is now so great that choices will have to be made based on more rational criteria of health gain than at present. The NHS currently rations covertly by 'deterrence, dilution, diversion and delay' (Ruddle 1991) and political interventions in response to media scares. Moving towards an open system needs a massive public education effort and public debate on the values that should underpin choice. That was Oregon's real if flawed achievement.

In Britain the debate has hardly begun and the context is very different. The British public expect a comprehensive publicly funded health service, and there is widespread dissatisfaction about the main form of rationing used: waiting lists. There is very little support for eliminating *any* treatment from the NHS. In a recent survey, 70 per cent of respondents were against restricting the provision of nonessential treatments (Davies 1991). When health authorities have attempted to do so there has been immediate and vociferous opposition, forcing a rapid reversal of policy (Salter 1992). The political task of leading this debate has been fudged because essentially it is so unpopular, but rationing, whether covert or overt, formal or informal, will continue to be a key issue for the future.

In conclusion, hopes that the 'outcomes movement' will become the 'central nervous system that can help us cope with the complexities of modern medicine' (Epstein 1990) expect too much from a promising development. Health policy cannot be reduced to a purely rational technical process even if the means were available. Nevertheless it promises better information to guide patients, guidelines for clinical practice and wiser decisions by policy-makers and purchasers of health care. In addition as the gap between the possible and the affordable becomes ever wider and societies grapple with the conflict between individual need and the collective good, the outcomes movement can at least inform the debate and as the Oregon experiment shows, begin to democratise the values on which choices are made.

Notes

1. Concern has been expressed by nursing organisations that some skillmix exercises have been undertaken in a simplistic manner, purely for cost-cutting purposes and with adverse effects on quality of care. Support for this view comes from a recent evaluation report undertaken for the Department of Health (Skillmix and the Effectiveness of Nursing Care 1993, Centre for Health Economics, University of York).

References

Banta, D.H. and Thacker, S.B. (1990) 'The case for reassessment of health care technology', *Journal of the American Medical Association*, 264(2): 235–40.
Beardshaw, V. and Davies, C (1990) *New for Old? Prospects for Nursing in the 1990s*, Research Report 8, London: King's Fund Institute.

Bosanquet, N. (1987) *A Generation in Limbo: Government, the Economy and the 55–64 Age Group*, London: Public Policy Centre.

Burns, T. and Stalker, G.M. (1961) *The Management of Innovation*, London: Tavistock.

Callender, C. and Pearson, R. (1989) 'Managing in the 1990s: the challenge of demographic change', *Public Money and Management*, Autumn, 9(3): 11–19.

Carr-Hill, R. (1988a) *QUALity Control: A Sensitivity Analysis of QUALYs*, York: Centre for Health Economics, University of York.

——(1988b) *The QUALY Industry: Can and Should We Combine Morbidity and Mortality into a Single Index?*, York: Centre for Health Economics, University of York.

Cochrane, A. (1991) 'The changing state of local government: restructuring for the 1990s', *Public Administration* 69: 281–302.

Davies, P. (1991) 'Thumbs down for Oregon rations', *Health Service Journal*, 14 Nov.: 10–11.

Department of Employment (1991) *Labour Force Survey*, London: HMSO.

Department of Health and Social Security (1986) *Mix and Match: A Review of Nursing Skill Mix*, London: HMSO.

——(1989) *Caring for People*, London: HMSO.

Epstein, A.M. (1990) 'The outcomes movement: will it get us where we want to go?', *New England Journal of Medicine*, 26 July: 266–69.

Ermisch, J. (1990) *Fewer Babies, Longer Lives*, York: Joseph Rowntree Foundation.

Fries, J. (1989) 'The compression of morbidity: near or far?', *The Milbank Quarterly*, 667(2): 208–33.

Green, H. (1988) *Informal Carers*, OPCS Social Survey Division series GH No. 15 supplement, London: HMSO.

Grocott, T. (1989) 'A hole in the black hole theory', *Nursing Times*, 85: 65–67.

Guardian (1990) 'Report reveals growing skills shortage', 14 Sept.: 17.

Handy, C. (1989) *The Age of Unreason*, London: Business Books.

Health Advisory Service (1983) *The Rising Tide: Developing Services for Mental Illness in Old Age*, London: HMSO.

Henley Centre for Forecasting (1991) 'Why companies will change', *Director*, 44 (8): 63–73.

Hogg, C. (1988) 'New medical techniques and the NHS', *Radical Community Medicine*, Summer: 35–41.

Hoggett, P. (1987) 'A farewell to mass production? Decentralisation as an emergent private and public paradigm', in P. Hoggett and R. Hambleton (eds) *Decentralisation and Democracy*, Occasional Paper 28, Bristol: School of Advanced Urban Studies, University of Bristol.

Hutt, R. (1989) 'Lasting the course', *Senior Nurse*, 9 (2): 4–8.

The Independent (1990) 'Scientist warns of a moral dilemma over gene therapy', 21 Aug. 1990, p. 5.

——(1992) 'Lasers set to replace the dentist's drill in five years', 19 March 1992.

Institute of Manpower Studies (1987) *'How Many Graduates in the 21st Century?'*, Brighton: University of Sussex.

Jennett, B. (1986) *High Technology Medicine: Benefits and Burdens*, Oxford: Oxford University Press.

Klein, R. (1987) 'A blurring of boundaries and diffusion of power', *British Medical Association News Review*, March: 18–21.

——(1992) 'Warning signals from Oregon', *British Medical Journal*, 304: 1457–58.

Loomes, G. and McKenzie,   (1989) 'The use of QUALYs in health care decision-making', *Social Scie,.ce and Medicine* 28(4): 299–308.

Maynard, A. (1990) 'Down with morbidity', *Health Service Journal*, 20 Sept.: 1393.

Means, R. (1988) 'Council housing, tenure polarisation and older people in two contrasting localities', *Ageing and Society*, 8(4): 395–421.

Mersey RHA/Nuffield Institute for Health Services (1989) *But Who Will Make the Beds?: A Research-based Strategy for Ward Nursing Skills in the 1990s*, Leeds: Nuffield Institute for Health Services, University of Leeds.

Mulkay, M., Ashmore, M. and Pinch, T. (1987) 'Measuring the quality of life: a sociological invention concerning the application of economics to health care', *Sociology*, 21(4): 541–64.

Naisbitt, J. (1984) *Megatrends*, London: Futura Publications.

NHS Management Executive (1991) 'Information Systems – a strategic framework for the NHS', *NHSME News* No. 51, November, p. 6.

Robinson, R. (1991) 'Health expenditure: recent trends and prospects for the 1990s', *Public Money and Management*, Winter, 11(4): 19–24.

Ruddle, S. (1991) *Rationing Resources in the NHS*, Southampton: Institute for Health Policy Studies, University of Southampton.

Rustin, M. (1989) 'The politics of post-Fordism: or the Trouble with "New Times"', *New Left Review*, 21 July, 55–77.

Salter, B. (1992) 'Heart of the matter', *Health Service Journal*, 1 Oct.: 30–31.

Sayer, A. (1989) 'Post-Fordism in question', *International Journal of Urban and Regional Research*, 13(4): 666–95.

Stiller, C.R. (1989) 'High-tech medicine and the control of health care costs', *Canadian Medical Association Journal*, 140: 905–8.

Stocking, B. (1991) 'Blinded by the reforms?', *Health Service Journal*, 3 January, 101(5232): 8.

Thompson, J. (1987) *Ageing of the population: Contemporary trends and issues*, Population Trends, Winter, pp. 18–22.

Townsend, P. (1981) 'The structured dependency of the elderly: the creation of social policy in the twentieth century', *Ageing and Society*, 1(1): 5–28.

United Kingdom Central Council (1986) *A New Preparation for Practice*, London: UKCC.

Walker, A. (1980) 'The social creation of poverty and dependency in old age', *Journal of Social Policy*, 9(1): 45–75.

——(1987) 'Enlarging the caring capacity of the community: informal support networks and the Welfare State', *International Journal of Health Service*, 17(3): 369–86.

Wilson, G. (1991) 'Models of ageing and their relation to policy formation and service provision', *Policy and Politics*, 19(1): 37–47.

CHAPTER 4

Reforming the NHS: the Conservative record

In the 1980s the policy prescriptions of the New Right gained intellectual ascendancy not only in Western Europe and North America but in countries throughout the world. From India to Brazil, and including the new democracies of Eastern Europe, governments espoused free market principles, privatised their state industries and began to restructure their welfare systems.

Health policy did not escape this intellectual challenge, but policy prescription cannot be assumed to lead to policy change. Governments attempting to implement change in this area often encounter entrenched organisational resistance from powerful providers and from recipients of services who benefit from the status quo. The extent to which ideas and values actually shape policy change requires careful empirical enquiry. Radical rhetoric can disguise essential continuities in policy or simply provide a *post hoc* gloss to changes which were happening anyway.

In Britain the election of the first Thatcher government in 1979 heralded the beginning of an ambitious attempt to 'roll back the state' by a true believer in private enterprise and market values. What effect did this have on the NHS? This chapter examines the Conservative record throughout the 1980s up to the passing of the 1990 NHS and Community Care Act.

Creeping privatisation?

One way of assessing the government's radical intent is to examine its policies towards the provision of private health care. The new government quickly showed its enthusiasm for the private medical sector which was growing rapidly in 1979, and in 1980 Gerard Vaughan, Minister of Health, expressed the belief that it might grow to around one quarter of the size of the NHS. But the expansion which took place throughout the 1980s did so largely without direct government help.

Intervention was confined to abolishing the Health Services Board set up by Labour to regulate private sector growth, stopping the phasing out of pay beds and allowing consultants on full-time health service contracts to earn up to 10 per cent of their NHS salaries from private practice without any salary deduction. Previously they had forfeited two-elevenths. Another minor concession was lowering the income limits for tax relief on private health insurance to £8,500.

It seems hardly likely that these changes alone fuelled the growth in health insurance from 5 per cent of the population covered in 1979 to 10 per cent in 1987. More significant were public perceptions of successive 'crises' in the NHS and a desire for more choice over the timing of treatment and the 'hotel' aspects of hospital services.

Figure 4.1 Total UK private acute care expenditure: cash and real spending (1972 prices)

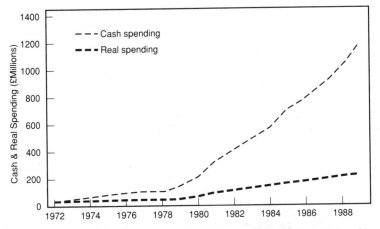

Source: Appleby (1992). Reproduced by kind permission of Open University Press, Buckingham

Figure 4.1 shows the growth in spending on private acute care in cash and real terms (after allowing for general price inflation) between 1972 and 1989. However, the most explosive growth in private health care occurred in long-stay residential and nursing care for the elderly (see Figure 4.2). By the end of the decade the voluntary and private sector had overtaken the statutory sector (local authorities and the NHS) as the main institutional provider, an expansion which had been funded largely out of social security payments. Rather than being the result of deliberate government intention, this reflected the unintended (and embarrassing) consequence of minor regulatory change. The Department of Social Security had always had discretionary power to pay for nursing or residential home care though this was little known. Klein reports that the total sums spent began a slow rise from the 1970s, reaching £39 million by 1983. In an attempt to prevent this slow creep the department asked each local office to set a maximum upper weekly limit for fees in their area.

The result was precisely the opposite of that intended. The maxima quickly became the minima. More important what had previously been a low-visibility discretionary payment overnight turned into highly visible as-of-right entitlement.

(Klein 1989: 218)

The result was a sharp rise both in the number of claimants and the fees charged by private homes, subsidised by the Exchequer to the tune of one billion pounds by 1988. The government began the attempt to extricate itself after a critical report by the Audit Commission in 1986, which led to comprehensive reviews of community care policies (Audit Commission 1986; Griffith 1988).

*Figure 4.2 **Private health care: breakdown by sector (total = £6535 m.)***

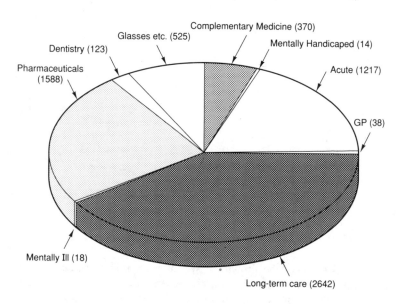

Source: Appleby (1992). Reproduced by kind permission of Open University Press, Buckingham

Large increases in prescription charges (from 20p. in 1979 to £3. 40 in 1991) also led to growth in pharmaceuticals bought over-the-counter privately. In some ways this was a symbolic move, since it raised little revenue: existing exempt groups (children, pensioners, the chronically ill and those on Income Support) retained their right to free prescriptions. In addition higher charges were made for all forms of dental treatment and new charges introduced for sight and dental checks.

The government encouraged the private sector in other ways. In 1983 district health authorities (DHAs) were asked to 'test the effectiveness of their domestic, catering and laundry services by putting them out to tender' (DHSS 1983a). Though the expressed aim of this policy was to improve efficiency, ministers went to considerable lengths to make sure that private firms could compete on favourable terms, in the end to little effect since private firms succeeded in gaining only one in four contracts by 1990 (NAHAT 1990).

But for a radical government committed to 'rolling back the state' these changes, though controversial, were not large. Unlike housing and education, health policies were remarkable for their continuity in the 1980s and the NHS finished the decade battered round the edges but largely intact: still the overwhelming supplier of health care in spite of the growth in the independent sector; still tax-funded and for the most part free at the point of use; still growing in real terms even though that did not keep pace with demand in the view of critics. The Prime Minister herself had reaffirmed her commitment to the 'founding principles' of the service in her speech to the Conservative Party Conference in 1982 as she sought to allay public suspicion that the health service might not be safe in her hands. By 1990 cash spending on the NHS was two and a half times what it had been in 1979, topping £27 billion and making the DOH the second largest spending department (NAHAT 1990). Why had ideology been tempered with pragmatism?

The costs of change

The devotion of the British public to the NHS continued unabated. The NHS consistently achieves high ratings in public opinion polls, irrespective of the party affiliation of respondents, and is consistently thought to merit extra public spending (see, for example Taylor-Gooby 1987; NAHA 1988). There is evidence too that people see the two sectors of health care as complementary rather than in opposition: they are happy to use private medicine for specific purposes but want a strong publicly funded NHS as the backbone of the health care system (Taylor-Gooby 1985). Public opinion buttresses and is shaped by a formidable medical and nursing lobby in the Royal Colleges, British Medical Association and the nursing unions which can consistently command sympathetic media attention. The political costs of abandoning the NHS were simply too high.

So too were the financial costs. Leaked 'think-tank' proposals in 1982 show that the first Thatcher government at least contemplated replacing tax funding by some form of continental health insurance. However these ideas came to nothing and when interest was revived in 1988, the advantages of the present system appeared to outweigh ideology once again.

The merits and demerits of alternative funding systems were widely debated in the 'alternative reviews' which accompanied the Prime Ministerial Review of 1988. In contrast to the secrecy of the official review these were valuable forums for informed and open debate, particularly those conducted by the Social Services Committee (1988) and the Institute of Health Services Management (1988). The weight of opinion and evidence bore out the view that 'Britain has one of the fairest, most effective and most socially accountable forms of cost containment of any country' (Barr *et al.* 1988: 11). Changing to some form of European or American insurance system would significantly increase costs.

Nevertheless the government faced the same problem that every other government had faced with the NHS, trying to maintain a balance between a centrally controlled budget and escalating demands, demands shaped by the professional providers of services and the inescapable needs of an ageing population. But this government faced the dilemma from a different ideological perspective. Increasing demands on services estimated at costing 2 per cent more in real terms per year (Benzeval and Robinson 1988) were to be met by increased efficiency rather than by increasing levels of funding to match. There were two strands to the government's strategy, although 'strategy' is probably too strong a word for a policy which evolved opportunistically. The first was to recast management systems, structures, norms and values in line with the perceived virtues of the private sector, in particular its efficiency and dynamism (which Ranade and Haywood 1991 term 'privatising from within'). The most important element of this strand was the introduction of general management in line with the recommendations of the Griffiths Report (DHSS 1983b), which is discussed in detail in Chapter 6.

The second strand of the strategy was to tighten lines of accountability upwards. Under the headings of efficiency and accountability a number of initiatives were introduced which are briefly outlined below. Readers who wish to follow these up in greater detail have a number of good accounts to choose from (see, for example, Harrison *et al.* 1990; Klein 1989; Ham 1992).

The changes: a summary

The efficiency strategy: chronology of events

1979   The White Paper *Patients First* recommends abolishing Area Health Authorities and creating District Health Authorities.

1982   District Health Authorities go 'live'.
       Rayner efficiency scrutinies begin in the NHS.
       Accountability Reviews between Minister and RHA, and RHA and Districts start.

1983   Inquiry in NHS Management (Griffiths Report) published.

Circular on competitive tendering for the support services sent to health authorities (DHSS 1983a).
First Performance Indicators package.
Introduction of manpower targets.
Review of the NHS Estate.
Korner Committee reviewing the information needs of the service begins its work.

1984   Appointments of general managers begin. Pilots on management budgeting.
DHA reviews of units.
Minimum cost improvement programme introduced.

1985   Second package of Performance Indicators introduced.

1986   Annual performance review of RHAs by NHS Management Board.

1987   Introduction of performance related pay and individual performance review for general managers.
Resource Management pilots begin in six hospitals and six community sites.

1989   White Papers *Working for Patients* and *Caring for People* published.

The Conservatives inherited the recommendations of the Royal Commission on the National Health Service set up by the preceding Labour government in 1976 (Cmnd 7615). Its terms of reference were to look at the management of the financial and manpower resources of the NHS. Ignoring most of its recommendations the new government took a quick decision on one of the major ones, abolishing the area tier of management. The thrust of its White Paper *Patients First* (DHSS 1979) was to give new District Health Authorities (DHAs) more autonomy and devolve decision-making down the line to operational units (hospitals, community services). The government's new-found enthusiasm for decentralisation soon ended, however, as the department came under sustained Parliamentary criticism about the lack of accountability in the NHS and the department's failure to develop appropriate mechanisms to ensure it.

Two initiatives quickly followed. Annual formal reviews of performance of the 14 Regional Health Authorities (RHAs) by ministers and the DHSS began in 1982, and subsequently extended down the line, with RHA reviews of DHAs and DHA reviews of unit managers. In these reviews the performance of authorities and managers in attaining agreed objectives and targets is discussed, and new objectives are agreed for the following year.

The second innovation was the development of performance indicators. In the autumn of 1983 every health authority received from the DHSS a package of 147 indicators in book form to enable them to compare their performance against others on a regional and national basis on a range of quantitative measures. The indicators covered five broad areas: aspects of clinical activity, finance, the labour force, support services and estate management. The political context determined not only the timing of their introduction but their content as well: 53 indicators were related to finance, 43 to the workforce, 46 to hospital activity. There was nothing on primary care, few related to quality or outcome, none related to patient satisfaction or ease of public access. The primary concern of the DHSS was the cost and quantity of hospital medicine on which most of the health service budget was spent. Health authorities were asked to respond to the data they received and explain to their RHA any 'outliers', that is indicators appearing in the top or bottom 15 per cent of the national league table. Performance indicators quickly became used as a diagnostic tool to 'inform' the accountability reviews which in turn developed 'from departmental monitoring of broad strategies to deep monitoring of short-term operational plans and of control systems stretching right down to unit level' (Harrison *et al.* 1990: 129).

The introduction of general management was a vital mechanism for ensuring greater control and demonstrating to the Treasury, Public Accounts and Social Service Committees that the department meant to get a grip on the NHS. The final mechanisms for ensuring managerial accountability up the line were put in place by appointing general managers on short-term contracts, introducing an element of performance-related pay, and installing a system of individual performance review. By 1989 the DOH had installed 'a clear and effective chain of command' upwards from Districts to Regions, the NHS Management Executive and the Secretary of State (DOH 1989a: 13).

Attempts to make clinicians more accountable for the resources they used, another theme of the Griffiths report, led to pilot projects on management budgeting for clinicians, broadening out to a second phase of pilots in Resource Management in six hospital and six community sites in 1987. Other initiatives which formed part of the efficiency drive were the programme of Rayner efficiency scrutinies, the introduction of workforce targets, and the requirement that health authorities undertake sustained programmes of cash-releasing cost improvements (which included the programme of competitive tendering for laundry, catering and cleaning services.)

These initiatives were given extra impetus by reduced rates of revenue growth throughout the 1980s which forced changes in expectations and management behaviour. Increasingly funds for new developments had to be found from redeployment of services and savings. The annual growth in public spending on the hospital and community health services fell from an average of 3 per cent per year in real terms in the late 1970s to less than one half per cent per year for the hospital and community health services between 1980–81 and 1986–87 (Benzeval and Robinson 1988). The Family Practitioner services did better, averaging 3.0 per cent per year.

By 1988 the strategy of 'privatising from within' had forced considerable changes in the way the NHS was run. First, a new model of management had been introduced for managers to emulate, based on private sector practices and precepts. Second, the profile and responsibilities of management had been raised through the introduction of general management throughout the service. Third, the government had introduced new mechanisms to reinforce the accountability of health authorities and managers upwards, and shown considerable political clout in using these mechanisms to enforce its policies.

The government could claim with some truth that it had forced through changes in managerial behaviour so that concepts like efficiency, cost-effectiveness and productivity were accorded more weight in the organisational culture. The cost-improvement programmes had produced annual savings of between 1.1 and 1.5 per cent per year in real terms since they were introduced in 1984–85. The annual growth in the number of patients treated, at 1.9 per cent per year, was more than double the rate of growth in spending (Robinson 1991).

But the changes produced their own set of tensions and contradictions. The limits of introducing into the NHS a model of management based on private sector practices soon became apparent. Far from possessing similar freedoms, sanctions and incentives as their private sector colleagues, managers were subject to strong bureaucratic controls and examples of perverse incentives penalising good managerial or clinical performance were legion.

In addition, interpreting the activity statistics was impossible in the absence of any information on demand, need, quality of care and outcomes. Critics could argue that higher productivity was being achieved at the cost of pushing patients out of hospital 'quicker and sicker', and increasing the number of patients treated was still consistent with unmet need. This was partly for the reasons discussed in Chapter 3: more elderly people and medical advances which enabled more of them to benefit from treatments like joint replacement at even more advanced ages. The government found it impossible to refute such charges or change the overwhelming climate of opinion which believed the NHS to be seriously underfunded.

The funding debate

Although funding 'crises' are endemic to the NHS, the crisis of 1987 raised more than the usual political storm, and plenty of ammunition for the Opposition in the election campaign of that year. A survey of 106 health authorities undertaken by the National Association of Health Authorities in 1987 showed that most were facing severe financial pressures and taking emergency measures to meet them, such as closing wards on a temporary basis, cancelling elective operations, drawing on reserves and delaying creditor payments.

Evaluating charges of 'underfunding' is extremely difficult. Often international comparisons are used, with the charge that Britain spends less on health care as a proportion of gross domestic product (5.9 per cent) than any other country in the OECD apart from Greece and (marginally) Spain. Appleby (1992), however, has conclusively demonstrated the weaknesses of using international comparisons. Estimates based on demographic pressures, advances in medical technology and the costs of implementing new government policies (such as the introduction of new screening programmes) also have their drawbacks, but they represent a pragmatic way of estimating whether funding has been adequate to keep pace with demand pressures. Figure 4.3 shows the difference between actual and target funding for the hospital and community health services throughout the 1980s, taking these three demand pressures into account and allowing for efficiency gains (using cost improvement savings as a proxy for efficiency). Target funding is the estimated budget increase needed to cope with rising demands (on average 2 per cent in real terms each year) against which the actual budget can be compared, with shortfalls accumulated from year to year. The figures suggest that the crisis of 1987 which precipitated the Prime Minister's Review was the result of cumulative underfunding throughout the 1980s which could not be sufficiently compensated for by internally generated savings and efficiency improvements.

Figure 4.3 **Target and Actual Funding 1980–81/1990–91 Hospital and Community Health Service: England (1990–91 prices)**

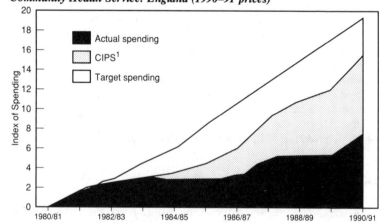

Note:
[1]CIPS = Cost-improvement programmes

Source: Appleby (1992). Reproduced by kind permission of Open University Press, Buckingham

In 1987 the NHS enjoyed its usual short-term electoral bonus, receiving generous settlements in the financial year 1987–88 and again in 1988–89 to blunt the edge of criticism. However, a review which was triggered by a crisis of confidence over NHS funding ended by saying nothing about funding levels at all and leaving the method of funding through general taxation unchanged (apart from the ideological blip of allowing tax relief on private health insurance for the over 65s). Instead attention focused on the delivery and organisation of health services. In effect the strategy of 'privatising from within' was pushed even further, by giving additional powers and freedoms to managers, introducing a quasi-market, and tackling a number of other organisational rigidities.

Strengths and weaknesses of the NHS

In the wide ranging debates which accompanied the Prime Minister's Review of the NHS, there was widespread agreement both on the strengths and weaknesses of the British health care system. It provides a reasonably equitable and comprehensive service to the whole population at remarkably small cost. Spending is easier to cap because it is centrally controlled, and because the allocations to health authorities for running hospital and community health services, accounting for 70 per cent of total spending, are cash limited.

Capital spending is rigorously controlled, and in general this has permitted a cautious approach to the adoption and dissemination of new expensive technologies (Stocking 1988). Administrative costs in the NHS were traditionally low, representing less than 10 per cent in the UK compared to more than 20 per cent in the USA. Furthermore, a well-developed system of primary care means that GPs can act as gatekeepers filtering demands made on the more expensive specialist and hospital services. The percentage of all medical practitioners in Britain who are in general practice is 46 compared to 12 per cent in the USA (Weiner 1987). Because medical practitioners are either salaried or paid on a capitation basis they have no financial incentive to 'overtreat', and the competitive bidding-up of salaries has not been possible when pay and salary structures are nationally negotiated (though this may change in future).

The weaknesses of the NHS were also well-known (see, for example, IHSM 1988; Culyer 1988; Klein and Day 1988), but the analysis and prescription of the American economist Alain Enthoven, written after a visit to Britain in 1985, was particularly influential (Enthoven 1985). Enthoven pointed out that whereas the NHS efficiently contained costs at the macro-level it provided few incentives to consistently reward efficiency and high performance at the micro-level, and indeed penalised both. Some of the main problems were:

1 Poor matching of funding to workload

Funding allocations to regions, and from them to districts, basically followed a need-based formula (known as the Resource Allocation Working Party formula or RAWP) adjusted for factors like teaching and research, funding for regional specialities and cross-boundary flows. Cross-boundary flow occurs when a patient resident in one region requires treatment in another. Within regions there are similar flows between districts, often of a substantial kind. The number of inpatients treated from other districts is more than 50 per cent in one district in ten. Most of these are teaching districts but one quarter of nonteaching districts had flows in excess of 33 per cent in 1988 (Brazier *et al.* 1988).

Compensation for cross boundary flows suffered from a number of flaws and disincentives:

a Compensation was not made in cash but only as an adjustment to a district's RAWP target after a two-year time lag.
b Day patients and outpatients were not included in the calculation although this may be the most cost-effective form of treatment.
c The formula was calculated on average speciality costs which do not take into account the extra severity and complexity of referrals particularly to teaching hospitals.

Hence cross-boundary flows, and the inability of districts to control referrals from general practitioners, were a major cause of the financial problems such districts have suffered in recent years.

2 Inappropriate incentives for managers and clinicians

Examples of inappropriate incentives for managers and clinicians were legion. For example:

a With cash-limited budgets, efficient authorities who treated more patients simply increased their costs, not their revenue (the efficiency trap). This often led to unused spare capacity, as beds were closed and surgeons idle towards the end of the financial year.
b A reputation for shorter waiting times or clinical excellence attracted more referrals but no extra money.
c A poor service meant that GPs referred patients to another district, and the district providing the poor service was rewarded by less work but no deduction from their budget.
d Clinicians who built up their NHS waiting lists created demand for their services in private practice. Their colleagues who worked hard to reduce their waiting lists only attracted more work.

Disincentives applied at the level of general practice as well. Cost-effective behaviour (prevention work, carrying out more minor surgery) was not rewarded, and GPs lacked information signalling the relative cost-effectiveness of different therapies and packages of care (Bevan *et al.* 1988). This resulted in wide variations in the range and quality of services provided (RCGP 1985), in the rate of referrals for out-patient, diagnostic and in-patient treatment and in prescribing costs per head. The effect of these variations on health outcomes is simply unknown.

3 Lack of responsiveness to consumers

It was a familiar complaint from right-wing analysts that the NHS was unresponsive to consumers, but as discussed in Chapter 2 they are not alone in this criticism. From rather different standpoints feminists, radicals and Marxists have criticised the paternalist and even oppressive nature of relations between providers and consumers of health care, and from the perspective of a businessman Griffiths challenged the NHS to become more aware of the needs of its users.

4 Few incentives to innovate

Finally, the disincentives to innovate are a familiar problem in public bureaucracies. The strong controls which are necessary to enforce public accountability for the use of taxpayers' money lead to caution, since experiments by their nature can fail.

What were the solutions? The government's answer had been to increase the responsibilities and accountability of management and put a good deal of political energy into the efficiency strategy. But this left unresolved the basic problem that 'those who take the decisions about what to spend money on are not the same people who have to account for it' (Gretton and Harrison 1988). Clinical domination of the service was still relatively intact and managers possessed relatively few formal controls over consultants, not even holding their contracts outside teaching districts. The pilot studies on management budgeting which tried to make clinicians accountable for a budget related to agreed workload targets demonstrated the difficulties of getting clinical cooperation on a voluntary basis and the massive efforts of persuasion and education needed for success (Harrison *et al.* 1989).

Enthoven's solution was not just better and stronger management but a structural separation of roles. The present monopolistic situation whereby health authorities assessed the need for services, supplied and managed them, and were responsible for monitoring efficiency and quality of care led to provider domination and provided no systematic incentives to perform well. It was, claimed Enthoven, as if '. . . we at Stanford said to students, "you can set your own exams and grade them" ' (Enthoven 1989).

The improvements that had taken place relied on the voluntary efforts of enthusiasts or political clout expended on particular initiatives. Inevitably this meant wide variations in performance, for example in achieving cost improvement targets (National Audit Office 1986; Haywood *et al.* 1989), in clinical productivity, and other measures of efficiency such as theatre and bed usage or rates of day surgery (Yates 1985, 1987; Audit Commission 1991). This in turn led to massive variations in waiting times and waiting lists, an issue of high public and political salience.

Enthoven argued that by separating the purchase of health care from its provision and management, and subjecting providers to an element of competition for contracts, providers would now have a financial incentive to cut costs, improve quality and be more responsive to what consumers wanted. Purchasers in turn, since they would still be cash-limited, would have an incentive to bargain for improved value-for-money. The government borrowed this idea of the 'internal' or quasi-market in *Working for Patients* (DOH 1989a) which was also recommended for community care by Roy Griffiths in his second report for the government (Griffiths 1988).

Further formal controls over clinicians were given to managers, but in addition the impersonal incentives of the market would, it was hoped, make doctors more cost-conscious and efficient.

Developments in primary care

Primary care did not escape the attention of the Thatcher government either. Here the aims were three-fold: curbing expenditure, raising standards and giving greater emphasis to health promotion and illness prevention. As the most individualistic and autonomous arm of medicine, general practice had maintained its position virtually unscathed since the National Insurance Act of 1911 established its main institutional features. The Act introduced the self-employed contractor status of the GP, care for a defined list of patients, the capitation fee and referral system and a medical record system still in use today.

The establishment of the NHS in 1948 represented the formalisation and development of the principles adopted ·in 1911, with general practitioners playing a pivotal role as 'gatekeepers' to the health care system. Apart from the agitation over conditions and pay in the mid-1960s which led to a new contract and the 'renaissance of general practice' the profession was virtually untouched by governments of either party, although the escalating demands on the hospital service which successive governments tried to grapple with were largely GP-induced. As Klein points out, GP referral rates increased over the history of the NHS, whereas the annual rate of GP consultations made by the public fell (Klein 1989). Demand was therefore shaped by the professionals rather than consumers.

Although no government willingly tangled with the BMA, it became increasingly clear to the Thatcher government that the financial costs of avoiding a confrontation with the profession might outweigh any political costs. Primary care was an obvious source of concern to a government anxious to control government spending. It represented an open-ended public expenditure commitment with no way of imposing cash limits on the amount spent on prescribing and seemingly no way to check the number of people GPs referred to hospital. In addition there was little evidence that increased investment in general practice was yielding any return, although in theory primary care should be able to treat many conditions less expensively than the hospital sector. The government also realised that an increased emphasis on health promotion in the GP's surgery might pay dividends, given the preventable nature of much modern morbidity.

The government's more active stance towards primary care began with attempts to control the prescribing budget through the 'limited list' in 1984. Vociferously opposed by both the profession and the pharmaceutical industry, compromises were made which both reduced the scope for potential savings and did little to impinge on clinical autonomy. Nevertheless an important principle had been established, that clinical autonomy did not mean an automatic right to use public monies without scrutiny or limits.

Further moves quickly followed. A consultative document in 1986 was followed up by the White Paper *Promoting Better Health* (DHSS 1987). The same themes of consumerism and better 'value for money' through stronger management which characterised policy in the hospital and community health sector are also reflected in government aims for primary care, with the additional aim of giving higher priority to health promotion and illness prevention.

Many of the proposals in the White Paper were introduced through the new contracts for general practitioners which took effect in April 1990, in spite of strong resistance. There are three main ways in which the government hopes to achieve its aims. First there are proposals to give patients a 'better deal'. GPs must provide fuller information on the services they provide through practice leaflets; Family Health Service Authorities (FHSAs), the successor bodies to Family Practitioner Committees established under the 1990 legislation, must publish directories giving information on the sex, qualifications, services and deputising arrangements of GPs in their area. GPs are allowed to advertise their practices subject to certain safeguards and arrangements for changing GPs and making complaints have been simplified.

Second, the services that GPs must provide under the contract have been made more specific to reflect the government's view of 'good general practice'. These include the requirement to provide health checks for all new patients, three yearly checks for patients not otherwise seen, and annual checks for patients over 75. The management role of FHSAs in monitoring the contracts, encouraging high standards and developing primary care generally is strengthened.

Third, the remuneration system became performance-related. By increasing the proportion of the GP's income derived from capitation fees from the average of 45 per cent to 60 per cent, GPs were encouraged to 'compete' for more patients by offering higher standards of care. There were also extra payments for doctors practising in deprived or isolated areas, target payments encouraging GPs to achieve higher levels of cover for childhood immunisation and cervical screening, and incentives for the provision of minor surgery and health promotion clinics.

In conclusion *Promoting Better Health* and its implementation through the new contract can be seen as the starting point for the subsequent reforms in *Working for Patients* (WFP). The Conservative government not only showed its willingness to challenge general practice and scrutinise its procedures and use of resources but also a strengthened commitment to health promotion. But the contract was imposed on an unwilling and angry profession, already alarmed by the publication of WFP in January 1989 and threatened by what seemed potentially strong curbs on their independence.

Working for Patients

Working for patients: summary of main proposals

The three main aims are to:

- Extend patient choice;
- Devolve responsibility;
- Secure better value for money.

The seven key features are

1 Devolution.
   All services currently provided by regions and districts not essential to their new roles should be devolved to lower levels of management or hived off into trading agencies unless retention is still the most cost-effective option.

2 Management changes.
   - At central level: A new policy board chaired by Secretary of State to oversee strategic direction of the service and a NHS Management Executive chaired by the Chief Executive to carry it out.
   - Regions and Districts: Health authorities reduced from previous 16–19 members to five executive members, (which includes the general manager and finance director) and five non-executive members appointed for their individual skills and experience by the Secretary of State/RHA. Non-executive members will be paid for the first time.

- Family Health Service Authorities: Membership reduced from previous maximum of 15 professional and 15 lay members to a maximum of 11 (five professional, five lay members and a chair appointed by the Secretary of State). Chief Executives to be appointed and management teams strengthened.
- Resource management: Implementation speeded up – all major acute hospitals could join the programme by March 1992.

3 Money follows the patient.
A weighted capitation system of funding replaces RAWP, phased in over five years. DHAs receive allocations for their resident populations and pay each other directly for services provided across their boundaries.

4 Self-governing trusts.
Hospitals and community units who can satisfy specified management criteria allowed to apply for self-governing status independent of health authority control. Trusts are run by boards of directors and raise their income from contracts won from health authorities, GP fundholders and private patients.

5 GP fundholding.
General practices who satisfy certain criteria may opt to hold their practice budget and buy a defined range of hospital services for their patients. Non-fundholding practices receive 'indicative' prescribing budgets monitored by the FHSA.

6 Purchaser–provider split.
In future the main role of DHAs will be assessing the health needs of the population and purchasing services to meet those needs, not the provision and management of services. The DHA is free to purchase services from its own directly-managed units, self-governing trusts, hospitals in other districts and the private and voluntary sector.

7 Medical audit.
- In hospitals: Local medical audit advisory committees chaired by a senior clinician set up in every hospital. Royal Colleges encouraged to make participation in audit a condition for a hospital receiving training approval, and audit participation will be a condition for gaining self-governing status.
- In primary care: Comprehensive system of medical audit for general practice to be in place within three years, supervised by medical audit advisory group accountable to the FHSA.

Many of the proposals in WFP reinforced changes that had already begun, such as resource management and medical audit, and were broadly welcomed. Proposals to strengthen management and subject clinical activity to tighter control also marked a consolidation of previous policies. Changes in the method of resource allocation also seemed to meet criticisms that RAWP funding did not adequately compensate for workload nor reward good performance. The DOH would be able to keep cash limits and the principle of making payments according to relative need by making weighted capitation payments to purchasing authorities, while money would go to the providers of services according to work done. More controversial was the decision to introduce the quasi-market: separating the demand for health care from supply and allowing limited competition between providers.

On the demand side, there were three categories of budget holder acting as purchasers of services for patients. As the main purchasing authority, DHAs were given the responsibility for ensuring that the health care needs of their resident population were met. After a transition period they would receive cash-limited allocations from the RHA based on the number and characteristics of their resident population and would be free to purchase services from within or without the district (subject to certain safeguards), from NHS, private and voluntary suppliers.

The second category of budget-holder were general practitioners. Eligible practices could opt to receive their practice budgets directly from the RHA. This included a drug budget, 70 per cent of practice team staffing costs, improvements to premises and monies to buy a defined range of hospital treatments for patients. (This was later extended to cover a range of community health services, see p.159.) The cost of these services was deducted from the allocation made to the relevant DHA. The third category of purchaser was private patients and insurers such as BUPA.

On the supply side, services would be provided by hospitals still directly managed by health authorities, hospitals and community units who opt out of health authority control and become self-governing NHS trusts, private and voluntary suppliers of services. DHAs were expected to devolve a substantial measure of autonomy to units who remained directly managed so that a clear distinction was made between purchasing and providing functions. Trusts were promised further freedoms such as the right to employ their own staff (including consultants), to vary pay rates and conditions of service, and to raise investment capital subject to certain controls. In the interests of maintaining 'fair competition' between public and private providers and the efficient use of capital, a system of capital charges was introduced into the NHS for the first time, and all hospitals were made responsible for meeting the interest and depreciation costs of their existing assets and new investment.

Contracts or service agreements are the method by which purchasers and providers do business. These set out prices, treatment levels and quality standards and enable purchasers to hold providers accountable for their performance. Cross-boundary flow adjustments to allocations will be replaced by direct billing for services rendered.

The quasi-market was therefore an attempt to expose providers to competitive tests of cost-effectiveness and quality while retaining safeguards for the consumer. It was a highly artificial construct with no precise parallel in any other health care system, and predictions about its performance were hard to make. The NHS was sailing into uncharted territory.

References

Appleby, J. (1992) *Financing Health Care in the 1990s*, Buckingham: Open University Press.

Audit Commission (1986) *Making a Reality of Community Care*, London: HMSO.

——(1991) *A Short Cut to Better Services: Day Surgery in England and Wales*, London: HMSO.

Barr, N., Glennerster, H. and Le Grand, J. (1988) *Memorandum of Evidence to Social Service Committee H.C 613*, p. 11, London: HMSO.

Benzeval, M. and Robinson, R. (1988) *Healthcare Finance: Assessing the Options*, Briefing Paper 4, London: King's Fund Institute.

Bevan, G., Maynard, A., Holland, W. and Mays, N. (1988) *Reforming UK Healthcare to Improve Health: the Case for Research and Experiment*, York: Centre for Health Economics, University of York.

Brazier, J., Hutton, J. and Jeavons, R. (1988) *Reforming the UK Healthcare System*, Discussion Paper 47, York: Centre for Health Economics, University of York.

Culyer, A. (1988) *The Radical Reforms the NHS Needs – and Doesn't*, York: Centre for Health Economics, University of York.

Dept. of Health (1989a) *Working for Patients*, Cmnd. 555, London: HMSO.

——(1989b) *Caring for People*, Cmnd. 7615, London: HMSO.

Dept. of Health and Social Security and Welsh Office (1979) *Patients First: Consultative Paper on the structure and management of the National Health Service in England and Wales*, London: HMSO.

Dept. of Health and Social Security (1983a) *Health Circular HC(83)18 Health Services Management: Competitive Tendering in the Provision of Domestic, Catering and Laundry Services*, London: DHSS.

——(1983b) *Inquiry into NHS Management (The Griffiths Report)*, London: HMSO.

——(1987) *Promoting Better Health*, Cmnd. 249, London: HMSO.

Enthoven, A. (1985) *Reflections on the Management of the National Health Service*, London: Nuffield Provincial Hospitals Trust.

Enthoven, A. (1989) 'What can Europeans learn from Americans about financing and organisation of healthcare?' *Healthcare Financing Review*, Annual Supplement.

Gretton, J. and Harrison, A. (1988) 'Stand up and deliver', *Health Service Journal* 19 May.

Griffiths, R. (1988) *Care in the Community: An agenda for action*, London, HMSO.

Ham, C. (1992) *Health Policy in Britain*, 3rd edn., London: Macmillan.

Harrison, S., Hunter, D., Marnoch, G. and Pollitt, C. (1989) *The Impact of General Management in the NHS*, Nuffield Institute, University of Leeds and the Open University.

Harrison, S., Hunter, D. and Pollitt, C. (1990) *The Dynamics of British Health Policy*, London: Unwin Hyman.

Haywood, S., Monks, A. and Webster, D. (1989) *Efficiency in the National Health Service*, Discussion Paper 24, Birmingham: Health Services Management Centre, University of Birmingham.

Institute of Health Services Management (1988) *Final report of the Working Party on Alternative Delivery and Funding of Health Services*, London: IHSM.

Klein, R. and Day, P. (1988) *Future Options for Healthcare* in Social Services Committee Session 1987–88 *Resourcing the National Health Service: Memoranda laid before the Committee*, HC Papers 284–IV pps. 48–51, London: HMSO.

Klein, R. (1989) *The Politics of the NHS*, 2nd edn., London: Longman.

National Association of Health Authorities (1988) 'Extra money for the NHS should come from taxation', *NAHA News*, June.

National Association of Health Authorities and Trusts (1990) *Healthcare Economic Review 1990*, Birmingham: NAHAT.

National Audit Office (1986) *Report by the Controller and Auditor General: Value for Money Developments in the NHS*, HC Papers 85–86 212, London: HMSO.

Ranade, W. and Haywood, S. (1991) 'Privatising from within: the National Health Service under Thatcher', in C. Altenstetter and S. Haywood (eds.) *From Rhetoric to Reality: Healthcare and the New Right*, London: Macmillan.

Robinson, R. (1991) 'Health expenditures: recent trends and prospects for the 1990s', *Public Money and Management*, Winter, 11(4): 19–24.

Royal College of General Practitioners (1985) *Quality in General Practice*, London: RCGP.

Royal Commission on the National Health Service (1979) *Cmnd. 7615 (The Merrison Report)*, London: HMSO.

Social Services Committee (1988) *The Future of the National Health Service*, Fifth Report, Session 1987–88, H.C.613, London: HMSO.

Stocking, B. (1988) 'Medical technology in the United Kingdom', *Journal of Technology Assessment in Health Care*, 4(2): 171–83.

Taylor-Gooby, P. (1985) 'The politics of welfare: public attitudes and behaviour', in R. Klein and M O'Higgins (eds) *The Future of Welfare*, London: Blackwell.

——(1987) 'Citizenship and welfare' in R. Jowell, S. Witherspoon and L. Brooks (eds) *British Social Attitudes 1987*, Aldershot: Gower.

Weiner, J. (1987) 'Primary care delivery in the United States and four Northwest European countries: comparing the ''corporatized'' with the ''socialised'' ', *Milbank Quarterly*, 65(3): 426–61.

Yates, J. (1985) 'In search of efficiency', *Health Service Journal Centre Eight Supplement*, XCIV(4957): 5.

Yates, J. (1987) *Why are we waiting?*, Oxford: Oxford University Press.

CHAPTER 5

Setting out to market

Introducing market-like mechanisms into a planned system of health care was never going to be easy. Against the timescales set by the government, that contracts for all services be in place by April 1991, it proved a stern test of general management.

The first important step was to separate the purchasing and providing functions and devolve services such as personnel and finance to units. This was complicated by the desire of some hospitals and community services to apply for self-governing status and achieve total independence from health authority control, which often led to local conflicts. Public suspicion that the real motives and intentions of the government lay in 'creeping privatisation' were particularly focused on trusts. The conflict was exacerbated by the politically inept way in which the issue was handled by the NHSME, with the chief executive writing directly to Unit General Managers (UGMs), 'inviting' them to express an interest in self-governing status, over the heads of their health authorities and often against their express wishes.

Preparing for contracts also imposed a massive management agenda on both purchasers and providers, requiring them to address the information deficiencies of many years in 18 months. Simply describing, assessing and costing the present pattern of services was a massive task, but in addition new information and accounting systems for contract monitoring, invoicing and capital charging had to be installed and capital asset registers compiled for every asset worth more than £2,000.

For their part, provider units had to think more like commercial organisations and acquire new skills in business planning, marketing, contract construction and negotiation. At the same time they had to continue running existing services, carry through any other major developments already in the pipeline and make progress on resource management and quality assurance systems.

The headlong rush to implement the reforms without pilots or experiments, when the information base was so poor, provoked much critical comment from observers (see, for example Social Services Committee 1990) as well as managers and professionals in the service (Appleby *et al.* 1991a). Enthoven himself had urged the case for demonstration projects to 'work at it till you work it out well in a few places – till you debug it' (HSJ 1989). The price for not doing so was costly mistakes and severe stress.

There was an alternative view, however, that forcing the pace was necessary if real change was to be effected. As one manager expressed it: 'If you want to move an elephant you have to be pretty rude about it.' The Griffiths Report had summed up the service's capacity for inertia and resistance to change just as graphically:

> To the outsider it appears that when change of any kind is required, the NHS is so structured as to resemble a 'mobile': designed to move with any breath of air, but which in fact never changes its position and gives no clear indication of direction.
>
> (DHSS 1983: 12)

Theorists of cultural change in organisations suppport the view that breaking down the 'disbelief system' which prevents acceptance of new ways of functioning calls for 'toughness, single-mindedness and even ruthlessness' (Richards 1989) before a 'new paradigm which will frame the organisational culture in future can be built'. However it was precisely this paradigm, symbolised by the Thatcherite language of markets and business, products and customers, that so many within the service found offensive. This was particularly true of doctors, the high priests of the old cultural order.

But what kind of 'market' was being introduced and how did it develop? The next section traces the traditional arguments for and against health care markets to set against the peculiar hybrid that was introduced into the NHS.

Markets and health care

In free market economic theory, perfectly competitive markets achieve an efficient allocation of resources by balancing demand and supply through the price mechanism. The assumptions underpinning the theory are that new suppliers can easily enter the market and there are no restraints on trade; that consumers are well-informed about their wants and the choices open to them and can exert leverage over sellers by threatening to take their business elsewhere. This creates the appropriate incentives for sellers to increase their efficiency (and reduce cost) and improve the quality or attractiveness of their products to buyers.

New Right economists such as Lees, Friedman and Selsdon have argued that the model, with appropriate modifications, is applicable to health care, which they deem to be a consumption rather than an investment good (the opposite view to that of Beveridge and the Fabian Socialists). The demand for health care, it is argued, is similar to the demand for any other commodity. Once consumers have to pay a price which reflects the real costs of providing health care, frivolous demand will be curbed and demand will be more likely to reflect perceived need (although there is considerable suspicion about the concept of 'need' in health care as distinct from demand). The absence of a price mechanism in state-provided health care distorts the relationship between demand and supply and forces a form of political or professional rationing which is more arbitrary and unfair than rationing by price. Consumers are not free to express their real preferences and suppliers are not subject to competitive tests of efficiency and quality.

The counter arguments, however, are that in practice health care markets are highly imperfect both on the demand and supply sides. On the demand side, consumer sovereignty is not possible since the consumers are not as well-informed about their conditions and treatments as the supplier. Demand is shaped by the suppliers themselves and ignorance makes consumers relatively powerless. Second, health care cannot be treated like any other commodity since health is a prerequisite for every other activity of living, and denying appropriate care to those unable to pay is morally unacceptable. (In practice, of course, a good deal of health care is either inappropriate, useless or positively harmful.) The uncertainty of catastrophic or chronic illness and the costs incurred means that no developed country leaves health care entirely to the market, even in the United States which most nearly fits the New Right model. Consumers pay either through insurance or income tax for health services, hence there is no true test of the New Right model of suppliers reacting directly to consumer preferences in the market place. The choice is between a national system of health care and some form of insurance with extensive government subsidies to those 'bad risks' – the poor, elderly and chronically ill – who cannot get cover. As Bosanquet (1983) points out, this in itself suggests that the relationship between demand and need is not as close as some New Right economists believe, and in any case introduces a very different set of arguments about the relative advantages and disadvantages of both systems.

On the supply side, there are two main sources of market failure. First, the relative powerlessness of the patient in the face of the doctor's superior knowledge can be exploited, particularly if the doctor has a direct financial interest in the outcome (the 'overtreatment' problem, for example). This is tackled through the ethical system of values socialised into doctors through the long process of training and, in many countries, by trying to break the link between clinical decision-making and the financial self-interest of the doctor, through third-party payment or salaried service.

Second, competition is difficult to ensure, giving scope for monopolistic abuse. Health care markets are not easily 'contestable' (Baumol 1982) since there are many barriers to entry against potential new suppliers, for example the heavy costs of new hospital development and technologies, and the legal monopoly given to doctors controlling entry to the profession.

To these traditional criticisms can be added more recent ones. There is no guarantee that competitive markets and more direct consumer choice lead to a more efficient and effective deployment of health care resources. The evidence from America suggests the reverse, with the inappropriate overuse and duplication of expensive treatments and technologies and a lop-sided emphasis on individualistic curative medicine at the expense of population-based prevention and public health.

Managed competition and the NHS

The present reforms attempt to gain some of the advantages of markets within a public health system, without their inequities and inefficiencies, by a managed form of competition. The system retains the principle of funding from general taxation, with treatment largely free at the point of use, and not on the ability to pay.

Separating the purchase of health care from its provision created the network of buyers and sellers, the necessary first step for a market to operate. The supply side of the market was opened up to competition, but on the demand side direct consumer choice was limited to the choice of a GP. Instead DHAs and GP fundholders continue to act as the agents of patients, purchasing services on their behalf.

To achieve the benefits of competition, purchasers could, in Enthoven's words: 'buy services from producers who offered good value. They could use the possibility of buying outside as bargaining leverage to get better performance from their own provider' (Enthoven 1985: 40). There were other advantages of the new arrangements which derived from the greater clarity of trading roles. Through their contracts purchasers would start to identify what services were being provided, by whom and at what cost and quality. In principle this should enhance the accountability of providers – both managers and clinicians.

In addition the strategic role of the health authority in assessing the health needs of their population, and purchasing services to meet them, gave them the opportunity of restructuring services in ways which produce greater net benefit. This might mean changing present priorities, spending more for example on prevention and health promotion, and using outcome data more systematically to establish priorities, as discussed in Chapter 3.

In principle the integration of primary and secondary care should also be enhanced (although this could have been speeded up if the government had integrated FHSAs with DHAs from the beginning). For the first time DHAs have to consult closely with GPs, who retain their rights of referral to any consultant. If DHAs ignore their wishes and preferences when placing contracts, and GPs send their patients elsewhere, the DHA could be in financial difficulties, since it must still pay for 'extracontractual referrals'. GPs, therefore, both directly as fundholders and indirectly through their influence on the DHA, have greater power to shape the services their patients receive.

Realising these advantages assumes that DHAs do have bargaining leverage over providers, that they do have choices and that they are given the freedom to make them. It also assumes that providers are free to manage their assets and personnel to maximise efficiency gains. In practice choices are often limited and freedoms have been tightly controlled so far.

First, there are significant elements of spatial monopoly within the NHS since provision has been planned to avoid duplication and achieve economies of scale, for example, for regional specialities. In addition local managers and consumers put a high value on convenient local access to services (Ranade 1989, Appleby *et al.* 1991a) which restricts their choices further. Regulation was therefore required to prevent monopolistic abuse. This took the form of allowing trusts to make a maximum return of 6 per cent on assets, and arrangements to ensure that certain services deemed essential would continue to be provided locally.

The extent of local monopoly means that the majority of DHAs still have to deal with their own local providers and may have no realistic alternative for the bulk of their services. On top of that, purchasing power has been fragmented between DHAs and GP fundholders. While fundholding originally represented only 3–4 per cent of practices, the eligibility criteria now permit 50 per cent of practices to apply. Each fundholding budget removes approximately one million pounds from the DHA's purchasing budget. For all these reasons the bargaining leverage of purchasers in some districts may be reduced.

On the supply side the freedoms given to NHS Trusts were considerably less than promised in WFP. An important motivator for units to apply for trust status was the freedom to borrow from the public and private sectors to finance capital investment. As trusts are public bodies, however, trust borrowing formed part of the public sector borrowing requirement, and triggered close Treasury interest. In the event each of the 57 first wave trusts found their borrowing limits – known as 'external financing limits' – set in such a way that their ability to raise capital was tightly controlled. This continued with the 103 second wave trusts. Trusts' freedoms to set their own pay and conditions were also modified. For example, to conciliate the BMA the government ruled that trusts must stick to central junior doctor staffing levels and pay staff at nationally negotiated rates.

DHAs have also found their freedom to make service changes heavily restricted by the political need to ensure stability in a pre-election period, slow down the changes and prevent disruption. Tighter regulation by Regional Health Authorities followed a much publicised role-playing exercise on contracting in the East Anglian

Region known as the Rubber Windmill (East Anglian RHA/Office for Public Management 1990). Under a tightening financial screw the market crashed in three days (simulating three years in reality). Although deliberately designed to test the market to destruction, the results shocked the participants and the Department of Health.

Thereafter the tight hand of regional regulation ensured that the first set of 'block' contracts followed the previous year's referral patterns and volumes of work, as the DOH exhorted a 'smooth takeoff' and 'steady state'. Even into the second year of contracts, when DHAs were beginning to get better information on which to base changes in contracts, regional regulation is tight. The political problems that arise when changes do begin to happen were illustrated by the GP fundholders who had greater freedom than the DHAs. Some began to negotiate better terms for their own patients which led to accusations of a two-tier service.

Experience so far of introducing managed competition into the NHS therefore has thrown up a number of political, normative and practical dilemmas.

Setting the rules of competition

The logic of a competitive market is that inefficient suppliers are driven out of business. It is a logic of winners and losers. However given the extent of monopoly (and oligopoly) in the NHS, the power of professional groups to win concessions, and the political need to guarantee equality of access the government has been forced to set narrow rules within which competition is allowed. Yet the more heavily regulated the market is, and the greater the restrictions on the property rights given to suppliers, the less scope there is for the benefits of competition to emerge at all. Furthermore, regulation can invite opportunistic games-playing. Experience in the United States shows that suppliers can evade or manipulate regulations through collusion between managers and clinicians and purchasers are usually in a weaker position to verify the claims suppliers make (Light 1990) Effective enforcement is difficult and costly.

Limits to contestability

Second, although the government has tried to open up the supply side to competition, barriers to entry still exist both in terms of medical personnel and hospital construction. In the first case this could lead to a competitive bidding-up of medical salaries by the new trusts leading to an escalation of costs. A more likely development will be that doctors continue to top up their incomes by private work, and are offered more of this in trust hospitals (Laing 1991).

In the second case, public expenditure controls over capital development inhibit the entry of public competitors and the heavy sunk costs of hospital development deter private ones. Nevertheless the market for particular services (such as pathology or transport) may be contestable. DHAs are already finding scope for substitution. For example, in one district GPs could quote a price for performing minor operations like vasectomies in a local community hospital at one-sixth the cost of the district general hospital. Contestability can also be redefined in a public sector context to apply to hospital managements. The NHSME or some other regulatory body could replace hospital managements who fail to perform satisfactorily, or particular teams could bid to take over the management of a hospital or other services on a franchise basis (Culyer and Posnett 1991).

Consumer power and consumer choice

A third set of dilemmas revolves around the question of how greater consumer choice can be reconciled with the need for controls over the total growth of services to prevent an expenditure explosion. 'Extending patient choice' was one of the key aims of WFP, but in practice consumers have little direct say over where and under what conditions they receive care. Managers and GPs continue to act as the patient's agent, and the rationers of health care.

Health authorities have been urged to earn legitimacy for their contracts by consulting consumer interests closely, acting in their role as 'champions of the people' when setting and monitoring them (DOH 1990). Many authorities have taken this up with enthusiasm, and there has been an impressive increase in consumer research (Appleby *et al.* 1992). But consultation is not empowerment, and the results can be ignored in the absence of stronger mechanisms of accountability to consumer bodies. For example, Community Health Councils, the statutory organs of consumer representation, do not participate in the planning of contracts, nor inspect trust premises as of right. They are dependent on the goodwill of DHAs and trust boards.

Income incentives of trusts and GP fundholders

The financial incentives given to NHS trusts and GP fundholders restore a link, even if indirect, between the financial self-interest of doctors and hospitals and the patients they treat. This may undermine public service and professional values, substituting commercial ones. For example, the need to generate income may lead trusts to concentrate on more profitable areas of work at the expense of others, or to discriminate between different categories of patients – private and public, DHA patients and those of GP fundholders – and between patients from one district and those from another. Some districts are gaining monies as a result of the change to capitation funding and others are losing. Gainers may specify shorter maximum waiting times for their patients and be prepared to pay for new and expensive developments, which patients from loser districts in the same hospital could be denied.

GP fundholders are subject to a new set of perverse incentives which arise from the fact that in their case purchasing and providing roles are fused, not separated as they have been in DHAs. This makes them rather like Health Maintenance Organisations (HMOs) in the United States, which receive a fixed annual sum of money to provide health care for enrolled patients; the system subjects them to the same financial incentives and may lead to the same adverse effects. With a flat-rate payment there is a strong incentive to exclude or undertreat high-cost patients – the elderly, poor and chronically ill – which is known as 'cream-skimming' (Luft and Miller 1988).

Glennerster et al. (1992) report that these deficiencies of HMOs were well-known in the DOH, and the fund-holding scheme in Britain was designed to overcome the worst of the problem by limiting the potential risks. For example, the hospital treatments that GPs can purchase were limited to standard relatively inexpensive procedures which the GP could easily diagnose and cost; the costs a practice would bear for any one patient were limited to a maximum of £5,000 (after this the DHA picks up the bill), and finally entry to the scheme was limited to large, well-managed practices. As the DOH has become more confident, however, limits on size have been progressively relaxed (from practices with 11,000 down to 7,000 and now experimentally with consortia of practices as small as 3,000). Whether these safeguards are enough to prevent 'cream-skimming' is still unproven.

The costs of contracting

Finally, the benefits to be achieved from clarity of roles and greater accountability which accompany the separation of purchasing from provision may be achieved at the cost of much higher transaction costs between what are now separate organisations. Economists using 'transaction cost analysis' argue that markets are a more efficient way of allocating resources than bureaucratic hierarchies only when products are relatively standard, and when information on outcomes, risks and associated costs is relatively predictable and known. Where these conditions do not prevail – as in health care – writing, setting, and enforcing comprehensive contracts which try to predict all contingencies and deal with all possible risks becomes very difficult and costly (Bartlett 1991). In practice, of course, such comprehensiveness becomes impossible, and this provides fertile ground for opportunism or for sellers to try to over-protect themselves against risk which drives up prices.

Whether these adverse effects develop depends very much on how the relevant actors in the NHS market conceptualise their relationships. In market economics narrow considerations of short-term market advantage dictate behaviour. In the real world behaviour has more complex determinants. Many markets which exhibit some of the same characteristics as health care – uncertainty, risk and imperfect information – are characterised by long-term relationships between buyers and sellers, which are based on trust, track record and a reputation for quality of service and reliability. At the same time they have developed an agreed body of industry-wide procedures to regulate the risks both share (Chambers 1990).

Lessons can also be drawn from 'relational markets', which are characterised by long-term relationships between buyers and sellers, focused around product or technology development and/or integrated production and information processes. Chambers argues that this pattern which characterises companies like Toyota or Marks and Spencers achieves economies of vertical integration without unified ownership and makes it possible to combine the advantages of markets with the virtues of planning, since it gives a measure of stability to both parties. The repeated nature of transactions between the two parties puts a premium on trust, cooperation and reputation as the basis for exchange.

Clearly this model has considerable relevance in an NHS context, where in the majority of cases purchasers and providers are locked into each other for a large part of their business; the information base on demand, cost and quality is poor and transaction costs are potentially high. Nevertheless contracting does incur greater administrative costs in the form of new accounting and information systems and staff. The number of managers in the NHS increased nearly three-fold from 1989–91, and the number of administrative staff increased by 10 per cent (*Guardian* 1993), while investment in new information systems will run into millions of pounds (Hughes and Bayes 1991). It is too early to say whether these increases in process costs will be offset by other efficiency gains.

In conclusion, introducing managed competition into the NHS introduces a number of dilemmas, some of which admit no easy answer. Much will depend on how local managers and clinicians implement the reforms at local level. The next section examines evidence drawn from a three-year monitoring study carried out by the author and colleagues in the National Association of Health Authorities and Trusts. Two national surveys of District General Managers (DGMs) were carried out in November 1990 and January 1992, paralleled by surveys of all acute providers in the West Midlands Region with more intensive study of four case study districts in the same region (Appleby *et al.* 1991a, 1991b, 1992).

Managed competition – the evidence

The first set of surveys revealed considerable support for the main principles of the reforms: 85 per cent of DGMs described their general attitude to the NHS and Community Care Act as 'mostly approve with some reservations' and 6 per cent had no reservations at all; 87 per cent agreed with the separation of purchasing from provision; 88 per cent considered the reforms would make the NHS more business-like and that this was a good thing.

If anything Unit General Managers (UGMs) in the provider units were more enthusiastic. However only 55 per cent of DGMs (60 per cent of UGMs) thought the market concept would work successfully in the NHS, so there was an element of support for the purchaser–provider split which was independent of ideas of competition and the market.

Three-quarters of providers were confident that 'this unit can take on the competition' and two-thirds believed they were in good shape to do so. Nevertheless 68 per cent agreed with the suggestion that if they failed 'in reality this unit will not be allowed to close'.

The case studies enabled us to study the process of separation in detail, how the new relationship between district and units was perceived, and the approaches to contracting. The four districts covered a wide range of 'competitive' situations and circumstances varying in size, range of facilities, quality of capital stock, cross-boundary flows and the proximity of competition. The four acute hospitals studied also varied in the extent to which they were dependent on business from their own district, from 20 per cent in a teaching hospital which had a large range of supraregional specialities and dealt with over 120 districts, to over 90 per cent in a rural district general hospital.

At the time of the first interviews in June 1990 the authorities were grappling with the devolution of services to the units and the district's attempt to come to terms with the new role of purchaser. In three districts implementation was characterised by a corporate approach between district and units, since all were aware of the dangers of instability and fragmentation, and concerned to manage the changes to produce benefits for both sides. Even so, many respondents were surprised at how quickly the different interests of units and districts had manifested themselves:

'I think Unit PLC now.'

'There are already flashes of independence from the units.'

Relations were more adversarial in the other district but this reflected longer-term problems. This corporate approach as well as the 'steady state' requirements of the NHSME in the first year of contracting not only affected the district's attitudes to its own providers but also what they hoped to achieve from the changes.

In the first district (A) all services provided by its own units were deemed to be 'core' by the DGM and were to be supplied within the district 'come hell or high water'. This approach was influenced by the belief that the district existed to support the units who would be free to compete and increase their market share as long as this did not jeopardise work for their 'home' district. Both the district and unit team were confident that they could increase their share of the market, based on their entrepreneurial record, spare capacity and efficient units.

However corporacy became strained when the acute unit wanted to apply for self-governing status. The district believed in the benefits of decentralisation but not a complete separation, whereas the unit saw its interests in wider terms than the district, as a provider of regional specialities, and wanted complete independence to pursue them. By the second year however the district was reconciled to the idea as the dangers of instability receded, and the unit became a second wave trust. Relations continued to be close and cooperative but the district now identified more with its 'champion of the people' role, less with the protection of its own units. Hence, contract negotiations became more 'hard-nosed' according to the director of contracting, as the district sought to maximise benefits for patients.

District B's acute unit had a virtual monopoly of business from its host district and felt completely unthreatened by competition. 'We have no regional specialities and no speciality which logically we shouldn't have in terms of patient flows and the population served. No reason for anyone to threaten us or vice versa.' The district had a peculiar geographical shape which meant that one-third of its residents were treated outside its boundaries. From a purchasing perspective no-one seriously questioned the feasibility of changing existing patient flows substantially. Instead aspirations at both district and unit level were confined to making relatively modest service improvements and getting more control over the quality of care provided to their residents by other districts.

Although historically the district had good relations with its units, it was also very devolved managerially, and had two self-governing trusts in the first wave. The DGM felt quite comfortable about this and also tolerant about the trusts' sometimes misplaced attempts to establish their autonomy: 'After escaping from the nest they go around flapping their wings and hissing at people'. He wished all the units had gone self-governing to allow the district to concentrate on its needs assessment and purchasing role and predicted that the units might be expecting a cosier relationship than he anticipated. The district was quite prepared to 'tweak the unit's tail' by using competition at the margins to get better performance from its own acute hospital, and was aware that this would force the unit management to challenge its clinicians more forcefully than in the past. The district was determined to get action on long-standing problems, for example, reducing waiting times in certain specialities, or making clinicians travel to patients for outpatient clinics at a peripheral community hospital, rather than make patients travel to the DGH.

The district benefited from the fact that it had comparative information on performance from a large range of providers which enabled them to take a more detached view of the strengths and weaknesses of its own unit, even though it also increased the complexity of contracting.

In the next rural district (C), the DGH was the only acute hospital over a huge geographical area. It provided acute services for a neighbouring district without a DGH, and this already represented one-quarter of its business. The opportunities of providing innovative packages of care to rural communities were considerable and some individuals in the units were alert to them. However, the district did not provide a favourable context for realising these opportunities. District attitudes to WFP were pessimistic and cynical, which in turn led to a reactive approach to implementation. Despite having a virtual monopoly of business from its 'host' purchaser, the acute unit felt unable to compete successfully for GP referrals with providers on the periphery of the district because of their old buildings and facilities. In the end, they argued, this would make them no longer viable and a ripe candidate for takeover by another district.

There was a long legacy of poor relationships between managers and clinicians, district and units, which hardly facilitated a corporate approach to the reforms. The pace of change was desultory, and the district only began work on contracting under the impetus of the neighbouring district it provided acute services for. By the second year there was little noticeable change: the threats they feared the year before had not materialised, but neither had much progress been made except that the language of contracts replaced that of budgets and allocations. It was business as usual. This in turn reflected an insular culture, a product of the district's remote position on the periphery of the region.

Finally district (D) faced the most difficult situation of all. It was an inner-city teaching district with a large number of units providing a range of specialities on a regional and national basis. Its main flagship hospital had high average costs, relatively poor physical stock, and served over 120 districts. Guaranteeing the security of the acute units was the major preoccupation of managers, who were realistic about the competition they faced in maintaining 'market share' once resident-based funding was introduced. There was no guarantee that districts gaining funds would continue to wish to buy the same quantity of complex and expensive treatments that the unit specialised in.

Additionally, the district faced a merger with a neighbour and major restructuring of unit management. For this reason self-governing status was simply not on the agenda for any of its hospitals. The district made good early progress on separating purchaser–provider functions, needs assessment and contracting, and was involved in early negotiations with other districts on joint purchasing arrangements, but the disruption caused by the merger of the two authorities in late 1990 blocked this momentum. By the second year there was considerable disappointment that they had not developed the purchasing role as far as they had hoped. Apart from the immense raft of organisational and personnel change caused by the merger, this was ascribed to the fact that all the units were still directly managed, which caused conflicts of interest and confusion of role. The unit's financial difficulties were absorbing a great deal of the district team's time and energy, and the promising consortia development of the previous year had foundered as each district in the consortia sought to protect its own providers. In spite of their own self-criticism, however, from a comparative perspective the district had achieved a great deal, surviving a punishing change agenda and formidable financial difficulties. In spite of this there were many instances of innovation on the commissioning side, particularly in public health and consumerism.

The evidence from the case studies demonstrates that managers did not respond to market signals in simplistic ways. Local politics and policy agendas, management abilities and 'appreciative systems' (Vickers 1965), and the historical legacy of past decisions were the main determinants of behaviour. In general there was concern to protect the security of their own providers in the first year, to try to sort out the information base for contracting and setting up appropriate systems. No-one seriously contemplated changing patient referrals significantly even if this had been allowed.

This was confirmed in one of the survey questions, which identified 10 factors influencing decisions on where to place contracts. Factors ranked high (1, 2 or 3) were existing patient flows (93 per cent), GPs' expressed preferences (74 per cent), ease of travel for residents (40 per cent) and previous experience of the provider (39 per cent). Purchasers responded only weakly to market signals such as competitive prices (22 per cent) or the fact that a provider had 'a well developed quality assurance programme' (12 per cent).

By the second year three of the districts were moving towards what Ham and Matthews call 'real' purchasing: needs assessment, evaluating service effectiveness, establishing priorities and beginning to make changes in ways which take account of consumer views (Ham and Matthews 1991: 21). As these districts became more comfortable in the purchasing role, they were also able to take a more detached attitude to their own providers. Although corporacy and good relations were thought to be important, both sides acknowledged that conflicts of interest were bound to happen which had to be worked through by negotiation and bargaining. It was, in one respondent's words, a relationship of 'creative tension'. There are clear parallels from the literature on 'relational markets'.

Competition on price was used only at the margin to win benefits for patients, for example in awarding waiting list contracts. Instead purchasers were using their leverage to ask questions and unravel long-standing management or service problems. Getting more information on comparative performance also enabled them to ask the right questions, although it also demonstrated the continuing inadequacies of data.

The second survey (carried out between December 1991 and January 1992) also shows evidence of change. Nearly three-quarters of districts were planning to change their health care priorities as a result of their health needs assessment. Many were also planning to change their contracts: 62 per cent were planning to cease a contract that existed the previous year; 71 per cent to contract with a new provider; 50 per cent to reduce volume more than 10 per cent with an existing provider and 78 per cent to contract for a greater volume of care per pound spent. How significant these changes were in monetary terms is difficult to assess. The evidence from the case studies suggests that while change will occur it will only be at the margins, but this may be enough to achieve significant behavioural change in service providers.

There were also shifts in emphasis on factors influencing decisions on where to place contracts. Factors given a high ranking in the second survey were GPs' expressed preferences (80 per cent), existing patient flows (80 per cent), previous experience of the provider (46 per cent) and ease of travel for residents (40 per cent). Once again competitive prices were highly ranked by comparatively few DGMs (24 per cent) though the same proportion of respondents were experiencing problems in obtaining comparative cost data as in the first year. Only 7 per cent gave well-developed quality assurance a high ranking. Significantly, 81 per cent gave protecting their own provider units a low ranking, a marked change from the previous year and in line with the case study findings.

Whether marginal or not, 55 per cent of DGMs believe that a 'market is necessary to get the benefits of the purchaser–provider split', while nearly one-third do not. Clearly therefore a bare majority of DGMs believe that at least the *threat* of competition is necessary to exert leverage, even if, as the case studies show, they do not contemplate moving much business from their main providers.

Another significant development emerging from the second survey is the extent of joint working and collaboration with other agencies. This reflects government exhortations to develop 'healthy alliances' (DOH 1990) to overcome current boundary divisions between primary, secondary and community care (in effect reintroducing planning by the back door) and to enable more powerful purchasing agencies to emerge. Joint working is particularly marked in relation to FHSAs, perhaps reflecting the importance many regions have given to this. Over 80 per cent are working with FHSAs on information systems, needs assessment and service planning. Over half are also collaborating on consumer research service specifications and service planning. Given this level of joint working it is not surprising that 83 per cent of DGMs agree that 'it would be better all round if this DHA and FHSA merged'.

Two-thirds of DGMs report some form of joint commissioning arrangements for their 1992–93 contracts, of which 75 per cent are working with another DHA, 66 per cent with an FHSA but only 31 per cent with the local authority. By the second year of contracting, consortia arrangements and outright mergers between districts to increase leverage and pool risk became increasingly common.

Finally, how do DGMs perceive the benefits and losses so far? The most frequently mentioned responses in two open-ended questions confirm the rest of the evidence. Benefits are those accruing from:

1   The purchaser–provider split (clarity of role, focus on health needs, more patient-centred);
2   Closer working and links with GPs, users and other agencies;
3   Much greater emphasis on quality issues (81 per cent in the survey believe that contracting has produced quality improvements in services);
4   Better information leading to improved decision-making;
5   Increased provider accountability.

The most frequently perceived losses or problems are:

1   GP fundholding;
2   The greater administrative complexity and costs associated with contracting;
3   The effects of rapid timescales (stress, information uncertainty);
4   Some commercialisation of values;
5   Uncertainties surrounding future restructuring and the intense politicisation of the NHS.

Conclusions

The astonishing degree of variation which exists between health authorities makes any attempt to evaluate the reforms hazardous. Nevertheless the evidence available, partial and fragmentary though it is, suggests that the structural incentives which have been set in place are starting to operate in the way they were intended and present opportunities to make services more responsive to consumers and more appropriate to local needs. But managers do not respond to competition in simplistic ways and price signals, which are in any case weak, are usually ignored in favour of other factors which purchasers deem to be more important , for example GP referral patterns.

However this evidence relates to the early stages of the reforms, when the market had hardly begun to operate and control was tight.

What happens in future when the brakes are removed is unpredictable, since there are significant problems to overcome. For example, is there the political will to allow hospitals to close if purchasers decide to put more resources into primary and community care? Who will develop as the primary purchaser: GP fundholders or health authorities? These issues are taken up again in Chapter 9.

References

Appleby, J., Little, V., Ranade, W., Robinson, R. and Salter, J. (1991a) *Implementing the Reforms: A Survey of District General Managers,* Monitoring Managed Competition Project, Project Paper 4, Birmingham: NAHAT.

Appleby, J., Little, V., Ranade, W., Robinson, R. and McCracken, M. (1991b) *Implementing the Reforms: A Survey of Unit General Managers in the West Midlands Region*, Project Paper 6, Birmingham: NAHAT.

Appleby, J., Little, V., Ranade, W., Robinson, R. and Smith, P. (1992) *Implementing the Reforms: A Second National Survey of District General Managers*, Project Paper 7, Birmingham: NAHAT.

Bartlett, W. (1991) 'Quasi-markets and contracts: a markets and heirarchies perspective on NHS reforms', *Public Money and Management*, Autumn, 11(3): 53–60.

Baumol, W.J. (1982) 'Contestable markets: An uprising in the theory of industrial structure', *American Economic Review*, 72(1): 1–15.

Bosanquet, N. (1983) *After the New Right*, Aldershot: Dartmouth Publishing.

Chambers, D. (1990) 'Learning from markets', in *Building the Contract Relationship,* Conference Paper 1, London: Office for Public Management.

Culyer, A.J. and Posnett, J. (1991) 'Hospital behaviour and competition' in A.J. Culyer, A. Maynard and J. Posnett (eds) *Competition in Health Care: Reforming the NHS*, London: Macmillan.

Department of Health (1990) *Developing Districts*, London: HMSO.

Department of Health and Social Security (1983) *Inquiry into NHS Management, (The Griffiths Report)*, London: HMSO.

East Anglian RHA/Office for Public Management (1990) *Contracting for Health Outcomes, (The Rubber Windmill)*, Cambridge: EARHA/OPM.

Enthoven, A. (1985) *Reflections on the Management of the National Health Service*, London: Nuffield Provincial Hospitals Trust: 40.

Glennerster, H., Matsaganis, M. and Owens, P. (1992) *A Foothold for Fundholding*, Research Report 12, London: King's Fund Institute.

The Guardian (1993) 'Market is strangling NHS with red tape, MP claims', 7 Jan.: 5.

Ham, C., and Matthews, T. (1991) *Purchasing with authority: the new role of DHAs*, Kings Fund College Papers, London: Kings Fund College.

Health Service Journal (1989) 'A guru vexed by his disciples', 21 September, 99(5169): 1150.

Hughes, J.T. and Bayes, J. (1991) 'Managing IT – the introduction and adoption of new systems', *Public Money and Management*, Autumn, 11(3) 31–6.

Laing, W. (1991) *Laing's Review of Private Health Care 1990–91*, London: Laing and Buisson.

Light, D. (1990) 'Learning from their mistakes', *Health Service Journal*, 14 October 99(5148): 1–2.

Luft, H.S. and Miller, R.H. (1988) 'Patient selection in a competitive health system', *Health Affairs*, 7(3): 97–119.

Ranade, W. (1989) *To Market, To Market*, NAHA Research Paper 1, Birmingham: National Association of Health Authorities and Trusts.

Richards, S. (1989) 'The course of cultural change', in *Managing Health in the 1990s*, Health Service Journal Supplement, 27 April, 99(5148): 1.

Social Services Committee (1990) *The Government's Plans for the Future of the NHS*. Minutes of Evidence HC Papers 1989–90, 148–51, London: HMSO.

Vickers, G. (1965) *The Art of Judgement*, London: Chapman Hall.

CHAPTER 6

Transforming management

The job of a general manager has changed almost completely. I'm starting out now, three and a half years in, almost with a new job. That's why it's so exciting. I've got a new management team. I'm working with doctors in a different way. I'm working to new income and expenditure rules from next year. I'm thinking about marketing my services on quality and relating to customers in a way that I'd just begun to think of before but now it's come right to the front. So that's been the biggest lesson for me. Just how much things can change in a short space of time.[1]

These remarks were made by a Unit General Manager reflecting on his experience a few months after WFP was published. Many of his battle-weary colleagues, three years later, may regard his enthusiasm with some cynicism but most would agree with him that the nature of management in the NHS has been transformed in a relatively short space of time.

As discussed in Chapter 4, Conservative policies in the 1980s invested heavily in changing the responsibilities and style of health service management. This was part of a wider strategy throughout the public sector which was based on the simple ideological premise that the private sector had everything to teach the public sector and nothing to learn. But the model of management that lay at the heart of this strategy was narrow, both in its conception of what makes the management of public services distinctive and in the lessons it chose to draw from the business world.

The radical nature of the Thatcherite attack has provoked a fundamental reappraisal of the role and purposes of public agencies, and in so doing provoked fruitful rethinking on what kind of management in the public sector is appropriate for the twenty-first century, in view of the wider social, technological and demographic changes highlighted in Chapter 3 and their impact on work and organisational life. Such a debate of course is rooted in the values of the participants about the proper place and value of government activity.

This chapter looks at changes in NHS management in the Thatcher decade in the context of this wider debate.

The concept of organisational culture

The wide-ranging changes which the Conservatives introduced into public administration in the 1980s placed great emphasis on changing the culture of government agencies to effect improvements in performance.

Organisational culture entered the foreground of management concepts relatively recently, receiving an enormous impetus from the work of Peters and Waterman in their best-selling analysis of successful companies in the United States (Peters and Waterman 1982). It is an amorphous and difficult concept to define but powerful in its implications. In simple terms it covers the beliefs, values and assumptions which shape behaviour in organisations and are reflected (perhaps imperfectly) in structures and processes. The determinants of an organisation's culture rest in its origins and history, technology and environment, patterns of ownership and control. But organisations are not homogenous. Different departments or functions may have different cultures, structures and systems reflecting their specialised activities and ways of working. An accounts department is different from a marketing department. Similarly within a hospital the culture of the accident and emergency department differs from the long-stay geriatric ward.

In Search of Excellence – a summary[2]

In their study of 'excellent' United States companies drawn from a variety of manufacturing and service sectors, Peters and Waterman (1982) identify eight features of management practice and organisational culture which characterise successful firms.

1 A bias for action:
   - Project teams that tend to be small, fluid, ad hoc and problem/action focused.
   - High value placed on communication, learning and experimentation.
   - Tackling complex problems by shifting resources to where they are needed to encourage fluidity and action (chunking).

2 Close to the customer: Market-driven commitment to service, reliability and quality. Ability to custom-tailor a product or service to client's needs.

3 Autonomy and entrepreneurship: Commitment to innovation and experiment, decentralisation, the delegation of power and a healthy tolerance of failure.

4 Productivity through people:
- Valuing employees as people and as a major resource, who should be trusted, respected, inspired and made 'winners'.
- Organisational units should be small-scale to preserve and develop a people-oriented quality.

5 Hands-on, value-driven: Organisation has a clear sense of shared values, mission and identity, relying on inspirational leadership rather than bureaucratic control.

6 Stick to the knitting: The principle of building on one's strengths and knowledge of one's niche.

7 Simple form, lean staff: Avoid bureaucracy and complex forms of matrix organisation. Build commitments around projects or product division.

8 Simultaneous loose-tight properties: Striking a balance between central control and the need for autonomy. Core values are controlled from the centre, but autonomy is given lower down the organisation to permit action supportive of those values.

Management writers who emphasise the cultural properties of organisations argue that the main task of management is to integrate these subcultures into a reasonably coherent and cohesive whole, to build a corporate identity and commitment through shaping the beliefs and values which guide action.

Organisational culture has become a fashionable concept but has been forced to bear a heavier weight than it can sustain in explanations of organisational performance (as the recently declining fortunes of some of the companies studied by Peters and Waterman illustrate). Corporate culture is not something easily amenable to management control or manipulation. Part of its determinants reside in prevailing power structures and relationships which shape both the external environment the organisation faces and internal corporate realities. The cultural approach to organisations needs to be welded to a political analysis if these determinants are to be given proper weight. For example, Morgan (1986) encourages managers to believe that they 'enact' their own realities:

Our environments are extensions of ourselves . . . A competitive ethos produces competitive environments. Visions of recession produce recession. The beliefs and ideas that organisations hold about who they are and what they are trying to do and what their environment is like have a much greater tendency to realise themselves than is usually believed.

(Morgan 1986: 137)

But the degree to which we can control our environment is often determined by others as Morgan goes on to point out: 'We all construct or shape our realities but not necessarily under circumstances of our own choosing' (p. 140).

The culture of any organisation is shaped partly by the dominant groups within it, their values and interests, and in the health service this means the values and interests of the medical profession.

The culture of NHS management

The overwhelming evidence from research studies into NHS decision-making, summarised by Harrison, demonstrates that up to the early 1980s the culture of NHS management was shaped by their relatively weak position *vis-à-vis* doctors (Harrison 1988). Theirs was a supportive role, smoothing the way for professionals, finding the resources to allow doctors to do their job, buying influence through performing services and favours (Haywood and Alaszewski 1980).

Harrison argues that three other features characterised NHS management in this period. It was reactive, responding to problems and issues thrust upon it day by day, rather than pro-active in trying to shape the organisation's future at a strategic level. It was incremental in the sense that the objectives and performance of existing services and the way in which resources were used were never seriously questioned or evaluated. Planning was confined to decisions on how to use incremental additions to the budget. Improvements depended on the size of the increment, not on savings or redeployment of services.

Managerial behaviour was also introverted, reacting to actors and problems stemming from within the organisation instead of looking outwards to the needs and wishes of its users. Essentially this was administration not management, concerned with maintaining stability and the status quo rather than achieving change, with process rather than action and results. It had developed largely as a realistic response to a political environment shaped externally by the rules and conventions of public accountability and internally by the central position of doctors.

From consensus to general management

The managerial arrangements that Sir Roy Griffiths reviewed in 1983 had been put in place by the reorganisation of 1974. A key objective of the reorganisation was to shift service provision away from acute medicine towards the faster development of community health services for the chronically ill, and improve the 'Cinderella' status of services for the elderly, mentally ill and handicapped (DHSS 1976). To do this local authority community health services were transferred to health authorities and multiprofessional management teams were set up which tried to balance the power of acute medicine by upgrading the influence of primary care, community medicine and nursing.

Teams were appointed at regional, area and district level. Each team included a treasurer, administrator, community physician and nurse. At district level it included a part-time consultant and GP member elected by their district colleagues. The teams were to operate by consensus, each having the power to veto decisions, none with the power to impose. But the realities of medical power were relatively unaffected by putting community physicians and nurses on the management teams. Community medicine, with its basis in public health and epidemiology, had a comparatively low status in the medical pecking order of prestige, and the district post was in any case mostly advisory. By contrast the nursing officer and administrator were the managerial heads of large numbers of staff. But although nurses had acquired heightened managerial opportunities they were ill-equipped by tradition or training to take advantage of them and often simply managerially incompetent (Strong and Robinson 1990), an ineffective counterweight to the medical members.

The co-option of general practitioners and consultants into management was largely on their own terms. Most used their power of veto to protect their members' interests and those who wanted to take a more corporate approach to district policy-making had no power to commit their colleagues.

Acute medicine retained its traditional dominance and the DHSS almost openly acknowledged its inability to make central objectives stick when it watered down its projected growth rates for the priority services in *The Way Forward*, produced in 1977.

The 1982 reorganisation tried to simplify some of the worst complexities of 1974 by pruning the consultative machinery, abolishing the area tiers, simplifying the planning machinery and advocating greater devolution of decision-making to units of management at the level of hospitals and community services. But it did nothing to change the institutional stagnation which had been the result of consensus decision-making.

The diagnosis of the management problem in the NHS by the Griffiths team was speedy and incisive, taking the form of a 23-page letter to the Secretary of State. As business people and newcomers to the NHS (apart from one, Sir Brian Bailey, who was Chair of the Health Education Council), their views of the shortcomings of NHS management paralleled to a remarkable extent the findings of academic research as summarised by Harrison.

The report started from the premise that the problems of managing the NHS were very similar to those in other large service organisations. The NHS did not have the profit motive but profits did not impinge on large numbers of managers in the private sector either, below board level.

They are concerned with levels of service, quality of product, meeting budgets, cost improvement, productivity, motivating and rewarding staff, research and development and the long term viability of the undertaking. All the things Parliament is urging on the NHS.

(DHSS 1983: 10)

The reactive approach of NHS management is criticised implicitly:

(The NHS) still lacks any real continuous evaluation of its performance against the (above) criteria . . . Rarely are precise management objectives set: there is little measurement of health output; clinical evaluation of particular practices is by no means common and economic evaluation of those practices extremely rare.

(p. 10)

The insularity of managers is also sharply criticised: 'Businessmen have a keen sense of how well they are looking after their customers. Whether the NHS is meeting the needs of the patients and the community, and can prove that it is doing so is open to question'. (p. 10)

Consensus management had led to 'lowest common denominator decisions and to long delays in the management process' (p. 17). Two central problems were highlighted: the difficulty of achieving any kind of change when so many groups had power of veto over decision-making, and the lack of direction and leadership from the centre: 'units and the authorities are being swamped with directives without being given direction' (p. 12). The two main recommendations to meet these charges were, first to establish a Health Services Supervisory Board within the DHSS, chaired by the Secretary of State to strengthen policy direction of the NHS. A full-time multiprofessional Management Board would be created to implement its policies and the link between them was the Chief Executive who sat on both. The second recommendation was to create a general management function throughout the service to focus responsibility and give leadership and direction. By general management Griffiths meant 'the responsibility drawn together in one person, at different levels of the organisation, for planning, implementation and control of performance' (p. 11). Griffiths also envisaged a new style and approach.

The recurring themes of Griffiths' managerialism are action, effectiveness, thrust, urgency and vitality, management budgeting, sensitivity to consumer satisfaction and an approach to management of personnel which would reward good performance and ultimately sanction poor performance with dismissal.

(Cox 1991: 94)

Coupled with the introduction of general management throughout the NHS was a real devolution of decision-making down to units. Although the report was respectful of doctors, its underlying thrust was the need to assert greater managerial control over their activities, by making doctors participate in management themselves.

Their decisions largely dictate the use of all resources and they must accept the management responsibility which goes with clinical freedom. This implies active involvement in securing the most effective use and management of all resources.

(DHSS 1983: 19)

Management budgets for clinicians based on agreed workload and service targets were such 'a vital management tool' that the Inquiry had already set up demonstration projects in four districts.

The impact of Griffiths

In their evidence to the Social Services Committee on the Griffiths Report, Evans and Maxwell concluded that its most far-reaching and radical aspects were its proposals for the central management of the service, with its promise of a new relationship between the DHSS and local health authorities and the change from passive to active management (Evans and Maxwell 1984). This would not be concluded once general managers were in place but involved long-term and profound cultural change, a view which managers themselves endorsed (Strong and Robinson 1990).

Assessments about the impact of Griffiths have been mixed, hardly surprising in an organisation as large and diverse as the NHS. Best, for example, argued that changes had been immense: 'In just five years (the NHS) has been transformed from a classic example of an administered public sector bureaucracy into one that increasingly is exhibiting the qualities that reflect positive, purposeful management' (Best 1987: 4).

Evidence of change lay in the increasing local diversity of management arrangements as authorities and managers used their new found autonomy to shape structures and roles to suit themselves. This often entailed breaking down traditional professional and functional hierarchies and the creation of new 'cross-breeds' or 'clinically aware accountants and cost-conscious clinicians' (Strong and Robinson 1990). A shift towards devolving responsibilities to lower levels, the introduction of performance review for authorities and individuals, and a renewed interest in quality and the consumer are also cited. Two-thirds of management boards by 1987 included a senior manager with primary responsibility for promoting service quality and consumer relations. These were often displaced nurse managers who no longer had line management responsibilities at district level.

Above all, the new general managers appeared to be growing in confidence and authority, making decisions and taking action on issues which formerly would have been too difficult. The following interview extract vividly illustrates the perceived difference, in the eyes of one senior manager in an acute unit. He was commenting on the entrepreneurial style of his UGM who had entered the NHS from industry in the wake of the Griffiths changes (about one hundred appointments went to outsiders). This man had utilised an opportunity to integrate scattered obstetric and gynaecological services at the hospital site by building a new clinic. The anecdote is instructive for the light it throws on changing relationships with clinicians.

Manager: We sat with the clinicians and said, look we've got to identify the capital to do this properly and we drew up a clinic scheme and then we had to compromise on what they wanted and John at one stage said, 'I'm sorry, that is what you're getting. Not ifs, buts or maybes, that is what you're getting', and they moaned like hell . . . Yet they've got their own individual consulting suites, a colposcopy suite and an enormous waiting area, everything you want in a modern clinic, and yet they're still moaning . . .

Interviewer: What do you think is the reason for that?

Manager: I don't know. I'm firmly convinced that if we had been operating under the old style of management, making a consensus decision, the clinicians would have got to their clinical representative and said there's no way we want that – we want everything twice as big and gold-plated taps because patients will die, etc., and their rep would say, 'I'm sorry but it's completely unacceptable to my colleagues'. At that point the nurses would have said well, yes we can see the reasons because we're nearly doctors as well, and the administrator would have been left high and dry. There would have been no action and there'd have been a nice plan on the table and I sincerely believe that but for general management we would have lost the opportunity to (a) have got the money, and (b) got the clinic built before people could actually realise what was happening and there's been other instances of that.

However, other studies suggest that relationships with clinicians continued to be difficult and not all general managers exerted their authority as successfully as this one. Most consultants viewed management budgeting with suspicion, as a vehicle for cutting their budgets, and few were interested in time-consuming management posts (Harrison *et al.* 1987) while managers still had few powers of discipline or reward. By arguing that general managers would have to 'harness the best of the consensus management approach and avoid the worst of the problems it can present' (DHSS 1983: 17), Griffiths appeared to recognise the difficulties of managing a multiprofessional service while seriously underestimating the power of doctors in particular to resist being managed. For that reason it was probably in those districts where consensus management had worked well that general management succeeded most.

Relations with RHAs and the Management Board also failed to live up to the Griffiths vision of giving general managers local autonomy and freedom to manage within the context of personal and corporate accountability for the attainment of agreed targets and objectives. The commitment to devolution conflicted with a stream of top-down initiatives which continued to spell out not only what managers should be doing, but how. If management is defined as 'taking responsibility for the performance of a system' (Metcalfe and Richards 1987a: 37), then NHS managers were doomed to continuing frustration and disappointment.

In addition, central management failed to provide the clear

leadership Griffiths had hoped for. Managers were bombarded with 47 DHSS 'priorities', many of them contradictory but all of them subservient to the overriding need to cut costs. Balancing the budget dominated managerial agendas in practice. Short-term contracts, performance review and performance-related pay for managers meant that they had little option in accepting finance driven agendas (Harrison *et al.* 1990; Strong and Robinson 1990) For many districts, Griffiths's concern with consumer research, improving quality, and evaluating effectivness were driven to the sidelines even though Peters and Waterman's *In Search of Excellence* increasingly appeared on the bookshelves of general managers' offices.

The new public management

The developments taking place in the NHS were paralleled by much wider trends in public management on an international scale which had many similar features. Hood (1991) argues that two streams of ideas had contributed to its development. First was the economics of the New Right, which led in the direction of competition, user choice, and the break-up of multi-functional bureacracies into decentralised units (such as the 'Next Steps' initiative in the Civil Service). The second was a new wave of business-type 'managerialism' in the public sector, premised on an updated version of 'scientific management'. The components of this managerialism are given below:

1 Management tasks in the public and private sectors are essentially the same (the fundamental premise of the Griffiths report).
2 Management is an expert activity which requires appropriate training; it is not the province of amateurs.
3 Management is an executive activity, which requires considerable discretionary freedom (the right to manage) to lead the organisation and achieve change.
4 Managers should have clear goals and objectives against which their performance can be monitored, and payment and reward structures should be geared towards the attainment of results.
5 Performance measures should be quantifiable as far as possible (the development of performance indicators).
6 Managers should be outward looking, trying to satisfy the demands and needs of the organisation's 'customers'.

The belief that government performance can be improved by better management is hardly new. The 1974 reorganisation of the NHS was guided by similar views and several themes of the new public management can be traced back to the Fulton Report on the Civil Service published in 1968. This time however government attempts to bring about change have been more determined and enduring.

Public-private management: debating the difference

This section cannot do justice to the body of literature on the new public management which has emerged, but will focus on two critical

---

Scientific Management[3]

Frederick Taylor (1856–1915), one of the great pioneers of organisation theory, originally developed the concept and practice of 'scientific management' in the early years of the twentieth century. This rested on five principles:

1 Shift the responsibility for the organisation of work from the worker to the manager. Managers plan and design, workers carry it out.
2 Use scientific methods to determine the most efficient way of doing work, and design the worker's job accordingly.
3 Select the best person to perform this job.
4 Train the worker to do it efficiently.
5 Monitor performance to see that tasks are done in the prescribed way, and achieve the required results.

Time and motion, work study, and organisation and methods developed as the practical consequences of scientific management, the tools for detailed assessment and measurement of every aspect of work, and designing and implementing more efficient ways of doing things. Perfect examples of this approach can be found today in the standardisation of service and product found in fast food chains like Pizza Hut or McDonalds. Every aspect of the production process has been analysed and broken down into minute components, the most efficient procedures developed and allocated to specialised staff who are trained to follow them precisely.

Taylor's methods produced startling increases in productivity in manufacturing, underpinning the assembly line technology of car production for example. But they also produced massive alienation from work, as workers became no more than machines themselves and gains in productivity had to be offset by higher rates of absenteeism and industrial conflict. Taylorism was as much about exerting control over the workforce as about efficient methods of production, and in the process workers were robbed of all autonomy and creativity.

Almost the entire development of management theory since has been a reaction against the mechanistic view of organisations, and the narrow approach to human motivation embodied in Taylorism. As Morgan points out however, Taylor was probably a man before his time. Scientific management can come into its own when robots rather than human beings are doing the work.

themes. These are distinct for analytical purposes though in practice they overlap. The first has emerged largely from the traditional study of public administration and argues that transposing a model of management developed in the private sector will fail because public sector management is distinctive (see for example Elcock 1991; Pollitt 1991; Stewart and Ranson 1988; Flynn 1990). The differences are said to be the following:

Role and purpose

Profit and the rate of return on assets, it is alleged, defines the 'bottom line' for managers in the private sector. While increasingly businesses claim to fulfil social purposes as well, they will not survive unless they satisfy their customers profitably in the market place. Public organisations, on the other hand, have been created by statute to undertake purposes collectively determined by the political process. Often they have been created to meet needs or express values (equity, justice, retribution) not readily met or expressed by the market.

Freedom to manage

The fact that public organisations have been created to serve collective ends in the polity, rather than individual demands in the market place, constrains managerial freedom of action. Strategic management in the private sector tries to position the organisation to gain maximum competitive advantage, achieving the right product mix, pricing policies, labour costs, and so on, in relation to a changing environment. Public organisations do not have freedom to exit from 'unprofitable markets' in this way and may have limited controls over inputs, for example, hiring and firing policies, pay levels, and so on.

In addition more complex and diffuse forms of accountability hedge public managers in ways which have no parallel in the private sector. These include traditional accountability to parliament or elected councillors, the courts and regulatory watchdogs to ensure standards of probity, impartiality and due process; managerial accountability within the departmental hierarchy for results achieved, including economy and efficiency; professional or peer group accountability for ethics and standards, and finally accountability to the service user and the local community. Competing accountabilities, it is argued, lead to more complex conflicts of interest and value trade-offs for managers in the public sector.

Relationships with the 'customer'

Because public managers deal with a more complex set of stakeholders, deciding who is the 'customer' is often problematic. In DHAs, for example, it could mean another department, unit or external organisation, GPs, patients' relatives, prospective patients as well as the present ones. In addition relationships with users of services are more complex than in the private market and may involve an element of compulsion and social control (social work, probation, some aspects of social security). Many public organisations are monopolistic and 'exit' is not an option for the user. Pretending that Income Support claimants can be treated like the customers of Pizza Hut, that tasteful waiting rooms and 'customer care' training for clerks, desirable though they may be, alter the essence of the relationship, fools no-one.

Uncertainty of goals and performance measures

The goals and objectives of public organisations are often multiple, conflicting and ambiguous. The political need to satisfy diverse interest groups, build coalitions of support, take credit for 'success', means that both the goals of policy and the criteria of evaluation are specified in deliberately vague terms. In addition there are genuine conceptual and technical difficulties in assessing 'performance' in services like the NHS or education and this may lead to concentration on the measurable rather than the important (as the early history of performance indicators demonstrates).

Relationship between demand, supply and revenue

If business people generate greater demand for their products through good marketing, they can increase the supply and bring in greater revenue. The public sector manager's budget is politically determined: 'marketing' the service to generate increased demand leads only to increased costs and not (normally) to increased revenue. Choice and rationing become inevitable in the public sector, but who decides the criteria of choice – the manager or the elected politician? If the manager, argues Chandler, then democratic decision-making is undermined (Chandler 1992). But political decisions can conflict with 'good' management. One example might be the political decision taken in January 1991 that no one must wait longer than two years for an operation by April 1992, irrespective of clinical need. To meet the target, managers were forced wastefully to expend resources on the most trivial complaints.

In summary, these critics argue that the differences between public and private organisations are too great for 'generic' management to be feasible or desirable. Other commentators (e.g. Metcalfe and Richards 1987a; Gunn 1988), while recognising the differences, argue that they are overstated. Public and private can learn from each other, as their environments are becoming increasingly alike. The focus of their criticism is the impoverished model of management at the heart of the Thatcher initiatives.

In their analysis of the Financial Management Initiative in the Civil Service Metcalfe and Richards argue that the government's attempts to change management in government was based on the 'Taylorist' view that management is about the control of routine functions within the organisation. This requires well-structured hierarchies, ideally into distinct cost or responsibility centres, explicit objectives and performance measures to monitor results. It would, if implemented, 'have dragged British government kicking and screaming into the 1950s' and limited the role of public management to the 'programmed implementation of predetermined policies' (Metcalfe and Richards 1987a).

The model, of course, is quite consistent with the centralising tendencies of the Thatcher administrations, their distrust and suspicion of public organisations, and determination to exert control. It also reflects their emphasis on economy and efficiency (narrowly construed) at the expense of quality and effectiveness.[4] Many short-term economies were at the long-term expense of both efficiency and effectiveness. There was for example no concept of 'spending to save'. Good examples from the NHS are energy conservation measures and building maintenance. Both were neglected in the 1980s in the constant pressure to find cost-improvement savings, though the first would have resulted in longer-term economies and the latter will result in much bigger bills through cumulative years of neglect. There was nothing in this model either to inspire public managers to create the 'cultures of excellence' that Peters and Waterman had talked about, and that the Griffiths Report in part reflects.

More fundamentally, Metcalfe and Richards argue that the government's concept of management ignored issues of environmental change and uncertainty. Bureaucratic hierarchies and the role cultures consistent with them are valuable for ensuring consistent reliable results under stable predictable conditions but cannot cope with 'turbulent times' (Drucker 1981). Constant environmental change and uncertainty is the reality for most organisations today requiring different organisational forms, corporate cultures which reward creativity and innovation, and a rethinking of the role and purpose of management. Metcalfe and Richards point out that the strategic management literature has wrestled for the last 20 years with the problems of managing for results in unstable conditions, yet the lessons which emerge are just starting to be taken on board in the public sector.

In another sense, the boundaries between public and private are increasingly difficult to maintain. The creation of executive agencies in the Civil Service, competitive tendering and contracting out, the establishment of trading agencies by health and local authorities, 'opted out' hospitals and schools, all create new grey areas in addition to the forms of 'quango' which already exist.

Similarly Roy Griffiths was right when he pointed out that many management tasks are the same in any organisation and some of the differences that the public administration camp stress can be overcome. The cultural revolution of the Thatcher years means that managing for results, accountability for outputs, is rapidly becoming the norm in the health service and the new executive agencies. Performance indicators are becoming more sophisticated as managers wrestle with the problems of choosing and monitoring appropriate measures of quality and effectiveness. The problems are often more difficult but the learning curve is rapid.

So if public and private are increasingly converging in institutional form and environmental challenges, and many of the tasks are similar, what is the analytical distinction between the two forms of management? Metcalfe and Richards believe that it rests on public management's focus on structural problems. This emerges from the institutional features of modern government which are not unitary hierarchical structures but networks of interdependent organisations.

> The critical area of public management is the management of organisational interdependence, for example in the delivery of services or in the management of the budgetary process. Public management is concerned with the effective functioning of whole systems of organisations.
>
> (Metcalfe and Richards 1987b: 74)

Analytically, the distinction becomes important:

> in situations where attempts by individual organisations to pursue their own (private) aims independently of what others are doing is both self-defeating and counterproductive from the (public) point of view of the performance of the system of which they are the parts.
>
> (*Ibid* :74)

An excellent example of this in practice was the East Anglian Rubber Windmill exercise described in Chapter 5, demonstrating what could happen in the 'internal market' if all pursued their private ends regardless of the public consequences. This definition of role and purpose undermines even further the idea of management as control. Instead it highlights the political and culture-building roles of management, and the skills of networking, bargaining, negotiation, creating and sustaining commitment to a shared vision. In practice, as Barrett and McMahon (1990) demonstrate from their learning-network of senior health service managers, this is what good managers spend a great deal of their time on.

Rethinking concepts of public management

Taking account of this critical literature, how might concepts of public management be broadened to meet this new environment and new challenges? What dilemmas have to be resolved? The first step is to recognise the diversity and complexity of public organisations which require different managerial solutions. They cannot all be fitted into the same rigid framework. Processes of accountability have to be redesigned to take account of this diversity as well. Accountability must flow downwards and outwards to users of the service, as well as upwards to councillors and ministers. New accountability processes have to grapple with the problem of legitimising managerial autonomy and discretion (to achieve results) with the need to give real rather than fictional accounts to the various publics with which the organisation interacts.

A key relationship is that with elected politicians. Management in the public sector is a highly political process, operating in the full glare of political debate and public attention. Managing the interface between the organisation and the political process is a necessary and legitimate function of senior management which requires skill and training. Trying artificially to separate politics and management, or treat the former as an illegitimate intrusion, is naive. Business people who enter the public service often have unrealistic expectations about the relationship with politicians. Victor Paige, the first Chief Executive of the NHS Management Board, resigned after 18 months complaining of 'interference'. But sometimes politicians have to be seen to respond to public concerns, if they are not to hand ammunition to their opponents.

Ironically many senior managers in the private sector argue that their work is also becoming increasingly politicised and subject to the 'fishbowl' effect. This is one instance where public managers have something to teach their private sector colleagues, who might benefit from the traditional training of public administrators in policy analysis and political science (Chandler 1992).

Being clear about the social purpose of the organisation (in management jargon, its mission and core values), and using this to clarify the nature of its relationships with users and provide an ethical system of values to guide behaviour, is a key task for managers and politicians jointly. The blurred boundaries of public and private have created many new ethical dilemmas for managers and also increased the possibilities for corruption and misuse of public funds which can only be addressed by clear working principles and codes of procedure.

Politicians also need to respect the motivations of those who work in the public sector. Incentive systems should be designed to promote and strengthen the social purposes and values of the organisation. Many professionals and managers choose to work in the public sector because they wish to give service or believe in the core values of their agency. This is particularly true in the NHS: ignoring these motivations and designing performance incentives solely around financial rewards perverts those values, and leads to cynicism and demoralisation.

Finally, public organisations urgently need to enhance their capacity for social learning, creativity and flexible response.

Conclusions

The new public management has wrought profound changes in the culture of public agencies, none more so than the NHS.

Traditional administration has been supplanted by active management with its focus on results rather than process and year-on-year improvements in performance.

In the NHS, the changes put in place by the Griffiths Report have been intensified by WFP. The reforms have speeded up the pace of resource management (now being rolled out to all acute units), made medical audit compulsory and strengthened managers' formal powers over clinicians. More fundamentally, managed competition and the new system of contract funding means that clinicians and managers have a common interest in demonstrating to purchasers that they provide good quality, cost-effective care. All of these changes have undermined medical resistance to participating in management, usually through some form of clinical directorate system.

The narrow emphasis on economy and efficiency which characterised the Thatcher years has broadened into a search for effectiveness and excellence as the current enthusiasm for quality in health care demonstrates. Consulting with the public, 'empowering' those who use the service, is seen as a legitimate management task. Managing across the boundaries, building a shared sense of purpose and direction across DHAs, FHSAs, local authorities, trusts and GPs to provide a 'seamless pattern of care' is increasingly exhorted by the NHSME and backed up by performance targets and sanctions from RHAs.

Yet in practice there is a huge gap between the best and the worst of management in the NHS, and 'macho management' on Taylorist lines is still far too common. There are also new dangers and dilemmas when too facile conclusions are drawn about the generic nature of management. If no distinction is made between public and private the search for good management is subverted by the ideology of 'managerialism': the belief that managerial expertise is the sole legitimate criterion for decision-making in public organisations. As Chandler points out, this undermines democratic values and marginalises the role of elected representatives (Chandler 1992). This issue will be discussed again in the concluding chapter.

Notes

1 All quotations from managers and clinicians in this and later chapters have been taken from the 'Monitoring Managed Competition' case study interviews, unless otherwise stated.
2 Adapted from Morgan 1986: 61.
3 Adapted from Morgan 1986: 29–33.

4 Economy concentrates on inputs, efficiency on the relationship between inputs and outputs and effectiveness on the attainment of objectives or outcomes. These are discussed in more detail in the next chapter.

References

Barrett, S. and McMahon, L. (1990) 'Public Management in uncertainty: a micro-political perspective of the Health Service in the United Kingdom', *Policy and Politics*, 18 (4): 257–68.

Best, G. (1987) *The Future of NHS General Management: Where Next?* Project Paper 75, London: King Edward's Hospital Fund for London.

Chandler, J. A. (1991) 'Public administration and private management: is there a difference?' *Public Administration*, 69 (3): 385–91.

——(1992) 'Politics, management and liberal democracy', Paper presented to Political Studies Association Annual Conference, Queens University, Belfast.

Cox, D. (1991) 'Health service management – a sociological view: Griffiths and the non-negotiated order of the hospital', in J. Gabe, M. Calnan and M. Bury (eds) *The Sociology of the Health Service,* London: Routledge.

Department of Health and Social Security (1976) *Priorities for the Health and Personal Social Services in England*, London: HMSO.

——(1977) *The Way Forward*, London: HMSO.

——(1983) *Inquiry into NHS Management (The Griffiths Report)*, London: HMSO.

Drucker, P. (1981) *Managing in Turbulent Times*, London: Pan/Heinemann.

Elcock, H. J. (1991) *Change and Decay? Public Administration in the 1990s,* London: Longman.

Evans, T. and Maxwell, R. (1984) *Griffiths: Challenge and Response*, Evidence to Select Committee on Social Services, London: King Edward's Hospital Fund for London.

Flynn, N. (1990) *Public Sector Management*, London: Harvester Wheatsheaf.

Gunn, L. (1988) 'Public management: a third approach?', *Public Money and Management,* Spring/Summer, 8 (1): 21–5.

Harrison, S. H. (1988) *Managing the National Health Service: Shifting the Frontier?*, London: Chapman and Hall.

Harrison, S., Hunter, D., Marnoch, G. and Pollitt, C. (1987) 'The reluctant managers: clinicians and budgets in the NHS', Paper presented to PAC/ESRC and University of York, September.

Harrison, S.H., Hunter, D. J. and Pollitt, C. (1990) *The Dynamics of British Health Policy*, London: Unwin Hyman.

Haywood, S. and Alaszewski, A. (1980) *Crisis in the Health Service*, London: Croom Helm.

Hood, C. (1991) 'A public management for all seasons', *Public Administration,* 69: 3–19.

Metcalfe, L. and Richards, S. (1987a) *Improving Public Management*, European Institute of Public Administration, London: Sage.

——(1987b) 'Evolving public management cultures' in J. Kooiman and K. Eliassen (eds) *Managing Public Organisations: Lessons from Contemporary European Experience,* London: Sage.

Morgan, G. (1986) *Images of Organisation*, London: Sage.

Peters, T. J. and Waterman, R. H. (1982) *In Search of Excellence. Lessons from America's Best Run Companies*, New York: Harper and Row.

Pollitt, C. (1991) *Managerialism and the Public Services: The Anglo-American Experience*, Blackwell.

Stewart, J. and Ranson, S. (1988) 'Management in the public domain', *Public Money and Management*, Spring/Summer, 8 (1): 13–19.

Strong, P. M. and Robinson, J. (1990) *The NHS – Under New Management*, Buckingham: Open University Press.

CHAPTER 7

Questions of quality

All political parties have their own reasons for pushing the quality of public services further up the political agenda. The large urban local authorities which remain the last bastion of Labour power have tried to undercut New Right attacks by improving the efficiency and quality of their services, and becoming more responsive to their users (Fenwick 1989; Young 1991). The Conservatives under John Major tried to distinguish themselves from their Thatcherite past by stressing a commitment to quality public services. The Citizen's Charter became a centrepiece of their election strategy and a minister of Cabinet rank was appointed to oversee its implementation afterwards. The Liberal Democrats, as the first party to develop such a charter, saw their own ideas borrowed by both their rivals.

If the quality of public services has achieved a higher political profile in general, it has reached a positively frantic pitch in health care. A casual browse through the monthly newsletter of the NHS Management Executive reveals an almost obsessive preaching of quality lessons to health service managers. Of course quality of care has always been of professional concern in the NHS, but it was firmly placed on managerial agendas by the Griffiths management reforms in 1983 and given a substantial boost by WFP.

Apart from short-term political factors, there are deeper reasons why the quality of health care has become more salient to politicians, managers and health care professionals in most of the Western world. Some of these are related to the costs of modern medicine and the limits to which efficiency savings can be made in nonclinical areas. The efficiency drive in the NHS in the 1980s, for example, left the clinical heartland of medicine relatively untouched, yet there is tremendous potential for redeploying resources from less effective to more effective therapies. In this case quality and efficiency, far from being alternatives, go hand in hand.

Other reasons revolve around the changing demands and expectations of consumers and their agents. In 1948 an austerity NHS was born in an austerity Britain and people were grateful for what they received. It is no longer an appropriate model for a generation which has developed sophisticated and discriminating consumption patterns for other goods and services.

But discussions about quality in health care are characterised by lack of agreement about definitions and concepts and riven by struggles for professional 'turf' (Pollitt 1992). In addition, questions of quality in the British context are particularly difficult to answer because of the complexity and range of services provided by the NHS and the wide-ranging but incomplete responsibilities health authorities have for the health of their populations. The purpose of this chapter is to try and clarify these issues by asking: (a) what is quality in health care? (b) whose quality are we talking about? (c) how can quality be turned into a reality in the new NHS?

What is quality in health care?

The literature is characterised by a bewildering range of definitions. These vary in:

1 The level at which they are pitched, from the macro-level of the health care system, down to the micro-level of interventions with individual patients;
2 The extent to which they incorporate consumer views;
3 Which aspects of the service they focus on.

A widely used definition pitched at the macro-level is Maxwell's (Maxwell *et al.* 1983), which underlay the King's Fund quality assurance initiative started in 1984. Maxwell argues that quality in health care must include elements of the following:

1 Appropriateness: the service or procedure is one that the individual or population actually needs.
2 Equity: services are fairly shared among the population who need them.
3 Accessibility: services are readily accessible and not compromised by distance or time constraints.
4 Effectiveness: the services achieve the intended benefit for the individual and for the population.
5 Acceptability: the service satisfies the reasonable expectations of patients, providers and the community.
6 Efficiency: resources are not wasted on one service or patient to the detriment of another.

But such a comprehensive definition poses contradictions between the various desirable aspects of quality and offers no criteria for making judgements on the trade-offs between them. For example, various studies have shown that the effectiveness of certain clinical interventions is increased by specialisation and this is one reason for having regional centres of expertise for more complex operations or rarer conditions to ensure clinicians see enough patients to 'keep their hand in' and efficiently ration resources. At the same time, this reduces accessibility and may be less acceptable to consumers, who would prefer more local services.

Out of Maxwell's list, Shaw insists that the key issue is one of appropriateness. All the rest depend on this being present, for if a procedure is not appropriate to a particular patient's condition it cannot be judged quality care (Shaw undated). However, Koch argues that acceptability drives the rest: 'the ability to provide any service which meets the patients' needs or expectations, or is seen to make stupendous efforts towards this, will be a major quality predictor of success' (Koch 1990: 132). This stronger focus on consumer inputs like acceptability characterises British definitions in contrast to United States ones, which emphasise the clinical rendering of a fault-free service to individual patients (see, for example, Brooke and Lohr 1988). Pollitt (1990) argues that this approach was largely process-oriented but has recently shifted to outcomes (surgical mortality rates, unplanned readmissions, prevalence of cross infections) reflecting the demands of more powerful purchasing organisations and litigious consumers.

When talking about quality, there is also often confusion about which aspect of a service is under consideration. Avedis Donabedian, an American pioneer of quality assurance in health care in the United States whose work has been very influential in the United Kingdom, modelled quality as a dynamic relationship between structure, process and outcomes.

Structure refers to the inputs of tangible resources such as buildings, staff, materials, and so on, but intangibles such as staff morale could arguably be included (Judge and Knapp 1985).

Process comprises all that is done to the patient with these resources, both clinically (diagnostic and therapeutic procedures) and nonclinically (nursing care, 'hotel' services, etc).

Outcome is the result of these activities and the benefits (or otherwise) to patients at the level of the individual and the population. In practice little is known about outcomes in terms of the effects of care on the duration and quality of life and 'intermediate' outcome measures have to be used such as those mentioned by Pollitt (1992).

The relationship between structure, process and outcome is very unclear. Although a certain minimum level of resources is clearly necessary to achieve a good quality of care similar results can be achieved with very different 'mixes' of inputs (for example, a different staffing skill mix). The key factor here therefore is efficiency – achieving a given output with the best technical mix of inputs at the lowest cost.

The critical elements in process are appropriateness and acceptability. The appropriateness of clinical care is assessed by expert opinion on what is 'best practice', but often no consensus exists. Wide variations in practice are partly the result of ignorance about the efficacy of many medical interventions (Black 1986, Fuchs 1984).

Users of services find it easier to judge the nonclinical aspects of care which traditionally have been undervalued by providers.

***Changing trends in standards of nonclinical care*[1]**

Environmental Provision

From:	To:
Public	Private (bathing and toilet facilities, single rooms).
Large-scale	Small-scale (normal houses for mentally handicapped group homes).
Utilitarian	Comfortable (flowers, carpets).
Fostering dependence	Fostering independence (facilities for ambulant patients to make their own coffee and tea).

Institutional routines

From:	To:
Rigid	Flexible (patients are not woken up at a set time).
Imposed conditions	Negotiated conditions (patient given choice of times for outpatient appointments and inpatient admission).
Batch	Individual (staggered appointments system for outpatients).
Closed care	Open care (access to partner or friend in childbirth; open access/overnight arrangements for parents of sick children).

Staff–patient interaction

From:	To:
Impersonal	Personal (continuing care from some practitioner in pregnancy).
Autocratic	Consultative (patient participation in drawing up care plans with nursing staff).
Inducing dependency	Supporting autonomy (fostering self-responsibility in treatment, taking own blood pressure or medication).

Part of the sociological critique of Western medicine revolved around the way patients are depersonalised in the medical system, their anxieties, discomforts and fear ignored. Much of this critique has been taken on board and many improvements made. Although improvements are of value in themselves the effect these aspects of care have on outcomes (for example, the patient's recuperative ability), is poorly researched.

Finally the critical element in outcome is effectiveness but as already mentioned there are still big gaps in our knowledge of the effects of many procedures both at the individual and population level.

One way to bring these different aspects of quality together in a concerted way is through total quality management, discussed later in the chapter.

Whose quality?

Conceptual difficulties are underpinned by organisational ones. Who gets to define, measure and act on quality in the NHS is, according to Pollitt (1992), divided up along 'tribal' lines reflecting professional demarcation boundaries and struggles for control among competing groups.

Unlike a number of other countries (for example, the Netherlands, United States, Australia), Britain has no national body to oversee quality assurance in health care in a comprehensive way. The Health Advisory Service covers hospital and community services for the 'priority' groups and children but has no power of enforcement. The Audit Commission, which has been given an extended brief to audit all health service facilities under WFP, pursues one-off enquiries usually with a value-for-money focus. The unwillingness to move to some form of more powerful and comprehensive agency in Britain along the lines of the Quality Commission proposed by the Labour Party (Cook 1990) has left quality issues largely in the hands of the professionals.

Managerial involvement increased after the Griffiths management reforms in the mid-1980s. One outcome was the appointment of directors of quality assurance, largely from the ranks of displaced nurse managers. These directors were usually given responsibility for all aspects of quality except medical quality, which was left to the initiatives of the Royal Colleges (see, for instance, RCGP 1985; Campling *et al.* 1990) and the voluntary efforts of local groups of doctors.

Working for Patients put further impetus behind the drive for quality, emphasising the need to make rapid service improvements in the areas of greatest public concern, and this was followed by a letter from the Chief Executive of the NHSME in June 1989 requiring districts to:

ensure that its units develop systematic comprehensive and continuous quality review programmes. . . . Within these basic frameworks health authorities will be expected to include provision to cover three particular areas mentioned in the White Paper: appointment systems, information to patients, public areas and reception arrangements and customer satisfaction surveys.

(NHSME 1989)

The government has also stepped more boldly into the contentious territory of clinical standards by requiring every doctor to participate in medical audit and, at the instigation of the Royal Colleges, setting up a Clinical Standards Advisory Group at central level.

But early evidence of the implementation of audit and the battery of other quality initiatives in the NHS suggest that doctors, nurses, managers and other staff, not to mention consumers, still step delicately in a ritual dance which recognises established prerogatives and power. Pollitt (1992) compares the way medical audit is being implemented and the results used as against nursing audit, as a good illustration.

The Audit Cycle

Medical and nursing audit use the same cycle of activity, focusing on the delivery of care. Most types start with observing current practice, and comparing this with information on what was the expected or desired outcome. The next stage is to take action to address the difference between the observed and expected standards of practice. This in turn is evaluated and the process starts again until the desired standards are met or exceeded. Then the standards are revised upwards in a continual upward spiral of improvement.

The Audit Cycle

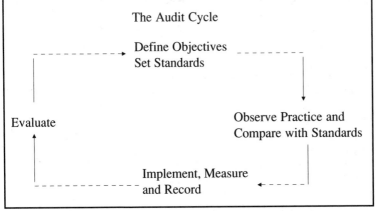

Medical audit was defined in Working Paper 6 as 'the systematic critical analysis of the quality of medical care, including the procedures used for diagnosis and treatment, the use of resources, and the resulting outcome and quality of life for the patient' (DOH 1989:

3). Medical audit was not new, and the Royal Colleges had been increasingly active in promoting various initiatives for some years. No doubt this reflected a genuine desire to raise standards but also reflected realism about growing political and managerial pressures for increased efficiency and cost-effectiveness. By demonstrating effective self-regulation the profession could fend off policing by others.

Pollitt argues that the model of medical audit promulgated by the leaders of the profession was designed to ensure that the process was 'a nonthreatening activity carried out only by doctors and rigorously protected from the public gaze' (Pollitt 1992: 4). Hence the audit process was entirely medically controlled, participation was voluntary, standards set locally and the results kept absolutely confidential. Doctors who regularly failed to meet local standards could not be disciplined by management, only by their peers.

To a large extent this model survived the WFP negotiations. The government conceded medical control without argument, hence:

The Government's approach is based firmly on the principle that the quality of medical work can only be reviewed by a doctor's peers. . . . The system should be medically led, with a local medical audit advisory committee chaired by a senior clinician.

(DOH 1989: 6)

Standard setting is not addressed in the Working Paper. In practice the Royal Colleges appear to have accepted that the wide range of local variation which exists is no longer tenable and national clinical protocols for the management of particular conditions have developed rapidly.

As for the principle of voluntarism, Working Paper 6 insists that 'every doctor should participate in medical audit' (DOH 1989: 6) but the careful language is designed not to offend: the words 'compulsory' or 'mandatory' are never used and Pollitt reports that the BMA were successful in persuading the government that no new disciplinary procedures should be introduced for non-attendance.

The principle of strict confidentiality still holds and discipline for nonperformance is still conceded to be largely a medical problem, not a management one. Pollitt points out that many managers do not agree but have not been disposed to make an issue over it so far. However there are ways in which determined managers can enter this 'hermetically sealed' process. First, it is up to them to ensure that 'an effective system of medical audit is in place' (DOH 1989: 6) and agree its overall form with the profession locally. This would enable a tough general manager to ensure that medical audit did not become simply a talk shop or token activity.

Second, the general results of audit have to be made available to managers so that they can take remedial action if necessary, which may mean initiating an independent audit. Third, purchasers can insist on seeing aggregate audit data, albeit in an anonymous form, to make quality comparisons between providers. This could strengthen the hand of managers in the provider units.

Where does this leave patients or potential patients who surely have the greatest interest of all in knowing about medical performance? Do they have a point of entry into this process? In general, no, unless they live in a district with particularly progressive clinicians. The Association of Community Health Councils formally asked for CHC involvement in medical audit in 1989 and were refused by the DOH on the grounds that it was a professional exercise (Pollitt 1992). Although 46 per cent of district purchasers report they are cooperating with their CHC on issues of quality, only 0.9 per cent included medical audit (Appleby *et al.* 1992).

Nursing audit incorporates:

the systematic and critical analysis of the planning, delivery and evaluation of nursing and midwifery services, in terms of their use of resources, the care delivered and outcomes for patients/clients, and introduces appropriate change in response to that analysis.

(Wilson 1992)

Nursing audit was already well-developed in the NHS by the time WFP was published, reflecting the prominent position nurses have taken in promoting quality assurance generally (Dalley and Carr-Hill 1991).

Pollitt (1992) argues that the application and development of nursing audit systems differ in important respects from medical audit, reflecting differences in professional perspective, power and organisation. In nursing, quality is largely defined by strict adherence to professionally derived standards, but this embraces the psychosocial care of patients as well as the physical and technical aspects of care. Hence there is more stress on the need to consult patients and take heed of their views. Recent initiatives like primary nursing and the pronouncements of the Royal College of Nursing (1989) take this trend further.

Nursing has a well-developed managerial hierarchy, unlike medicine, and nursing audit has usually been introduced and run by nurse managers instead of being simply a peer group exercise. Confidentiality is therefore not such a strong theme and the results of nursing audit have always been available to managers. This has led to intensive attempts to standardise costed 'packages of care' which bring together considerations of outcome with workforce and workload planning. Since nursing accounts for over one-third of NHS expenditure, the efficient use of this expensive resource is a prime concern of managers. Proctor's (1990) research illustrates nicely the conflicts which emerge between managerial and professional perceptions of 'quality' as a result of these endeavours.

The development of professionalism in nursing has led to an increasing emphasis on *individualised* care: adapting practice to the unique needs of each patient, enhancing the autonomy of patients in the organisation of care and encouraging independence. This requires a measure of continuity in ward staffing, to make sure that nurses and support workers know individual patients and understand the care plan. Managerial systems of assessing nursing workload and skill mix on the other hand (for example, Criteria for Care, GRASP) attempt to routinise nursing activities through work study methods, and link workload planning to assessments of patient dependency. Hence if the dependency levels on a ward increase, extra staff can be deployed. Proctor argues that this has led to an increasingly transient workforce on the wards. This undermines any attempt at individualised quality care since the workforce cannot assimilate the individual needs, likes and dislikes of a different group of patients each time they come on duty. Dependency on standardised routines and rough and ready indicators of patients' needs, such as their level of mobility, is essential (Proctor 1990). Recent work by the Audit Commission confirms that this is often the case (Audit Commission 1992).

Three important conclusions follow from this discussion. First, concepts of quality in health care are still determined largely by the professionals, with managers staking out an increasing role. Second, a shared view of what 'quality' means, which can underpin a commitment to organisation-wide strategies like total quality management, is often lacking. Third, 'consumers' – that is, patients, their families, potential patients – have traditionally had least influence over the kind of service they receive. Now WFP insists the consumer's views must be given more weight. Can this be made a reality in the new NHS?

Modelling quality in health care: a user-centred approach

There are good theoretical grounds for making the user's experience central to definitions of quality in a service industry like health care. Consumers judge quality by comparing the service they receive against expectations of what they should receive. Both perceptions and expectations are experiential states of mind rather than necessarily 'real'. For example, patients waiting in an out-patient department knowing that it will be 30 minutes before they are seen may be happier than those who wait half as long, not knowing how long the wait will be. In services like health care or education the experience of the user is the product being consumed. The behaviour of the consumer is also an integral part of the production process. For example the extent to which patients like or trust the doctor and nurse may affect their willingness to cooperate in their treatment.

Defining what the user expects and wants from a service however is complicated by the fact that perceptions change over time, according to where people are in relation to the system. They may feel differently depending on whether they are viewing the service before using it, encountering it initially, actually in receipt of the service, and finally in retrospect. Assessing and monitoring quality in health care will therefore require continuous interaction and feedback from users of the services at all stages of service design and delivery.

Quality and the NHS reforms

WFP offered two main mechanisms for improving quality, through the contracting process and through the systematic introduction of medical audit. However medical audit should be seen as part of a total approach to quality even if in reality it is often separated out. A third mechanism is also of growing importance: the Patient's Charter which was introduced in November 1991 as part of the Citizen's Charter initiative.

The contracting process – the introduction of contracts between purchasers and providers – provides an excellent vehicle for negotiating explicit quality standards and targets. A model of the process is set out in Figure 7.1.

Figure 7.1 **The Contracting Process**

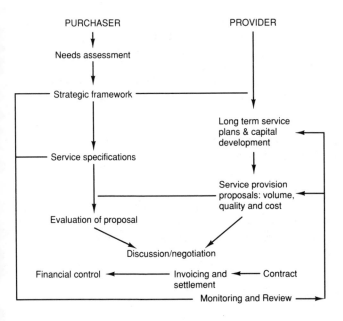

Ideally the system should work as follows. On the basis of their needs assessment, which includes consultation with consumer groups and GPs, purchasing authorities adjust their priorities in terms of the balance of resources which should be devoted to particular care groups, and the balance between health promotion, prevention, treatment and care. This feeds into the authority's strategic framework which sets out its statement of purpose, guiding values, aims and objectives in the medium term (usually over a three to five year period). At the same time providers will have their own development plans and ambitions and try to convince purchasers of their merit. Resolving the strategic aims of the purchaser and its main provider where these conflict may require difficult negotiations.

The service specification sets out the quality standards that purchasers expect. Increasingly these are at two levels: general service specifications which apply to all contracts and individual service agreements for particular specialities and services. Early advice from the DOH set out the quality aspects that contracts should seek to ensure. Appendix 1 shows the headings from the general Quality of Service Specification developed by one authority in the second year of contracting. By this time many authorities were developing increasingly sophisticated quality manuals and detailed standards.

Service qualities to be guaranteed by the contract[2]

1 The appropriateness of treatment and care.
2 Achievement of optimum clinical outcome.
3 All clinically recognised procedures to minimise complications and similar preventable events.
4 An attitude which treats patients with dignity and as individuals
5 An environment conducive to patients' safety, reassurance and contentment.
6 Speed of response to patients' needs and minimum inconvenience to them (and their relatives and friends).
7 The involvement of patients in their own care.

The specification itself will normally be developed in partnership with those providing services, both clinicians and managers. Providers then present their own service proposals which are the basis for negotiation and discussion, leading to formal contracts which are monitored and reviewed throughout the year.

Consulting the consumer

Purchasing authorities have been urged to listen to 'local voices' (NHSME 1992b) when assessing need, considering the placing and content of contracts and in monitoring and reviewing the quality of services. Recent evidence suggests considerable activity on this front. Consultation with GPs is especially close. In a second national survey of DGMs (Appleby *et al.* 1992), almost every DHA had met with GPs either individually or in small groups; three-quarters had held general meetings in addition and two-thirds had carried out some form of survey. Consultation with the public was less well-developed and took place largely through the traditional channels of voluntary organisations and patient surveys. Nevertheless 50 per cent had held public meetings, and one-third surveyed residents.

In deciding where to place contracts in 1992–93, DHAs put much weight on the opinions of GPs, but not on the opinions of the public. 'GPs' expressed preferences' was the most highly ranked factor: ranked low were the results of consumer surveys, the views of CHCs, and the fact that providers carried out regular patient satisfaction surveys. Realistically the scope for change in 1992–93 was low but it will be interesting to see whether the present flurries of consultation bear fruit in future or are simply a public relations exercise.

The survey (Appleby *et al.* 1992) does not explore consumer inputs into quality specifications and monitoring but the case studies suggest the following main methods:

1 CHC representation on quality planning and steering groups;
2 Patient/public surveys, often with CHC support;
3 Focus groups;
4 Regular consumer groups of users of specific services and relatives.

Newcastle DHA is one example of an authority taking an innovatory approach to consumer consultation (Barker 1991). A number of consumer groups have been established who have specific remits to review quality measures in contracts, and advise on changes. The Mental Health Consumer Group is particularly well-established. It began as a joint initiative between purchaser and provider with 15 users of mental health services and their carers. They have since developed a wide range of contacts and membership to the group is now by election. The group has a paid facilitator, and members receive a small honorarium on the principle that their time is valued. So far the group has systematically visited all wards and departments in the Mental Health Trust as part of the quality monitoring arrangements, identified a number of quality improvement priorities and commented on quality measures in the specification which has led to revisions. This model of consumer input is clearly not cost-free and is being carefully evaluated. Meanwhile a number of less formalised groups have been formed to advise on physical disability, learning difficulties (separate groups for users and carers) and HIV/AIDs. Even at this early stage it seems clear that different models of participation are appropriate for different types of service user, and experiment is necessary to find a form with which users are comfortable.

Focus groups have been tried on acute wards with patients recuperating from operations who are able and willing to participate. Though popular with patients, such a departure from traditional practice has been known to outrage consultants, demanding to know what the researcher is doing with their patients!

Total quality management

Total quality management (TQM) is the currently fashionable approach to quality improvement in the health service, adopted from the lessons of Japanese industry and the exhortations of management gurus like Tom Peters. Its key tenets are:

1 The customer comes first: The first and most important characteristic of total quality is the search continually to meet, and even exceed, the customer's demands and expectations.
2 Corporate commitment and planning: TQM requires a particular kind of strategic leadership which can provide the vision and commitment, plan for change and see that it is implemented (Peters and Austin 1985). Peters talks of the obsession with quality which characterised many leaders in the 'excellent company' research.
3 Everyone participates in TQM: Quality must become everyone's business, not just that of top management or quality specialists. Everyone has customers, even though these are internal to the organisation, and many quality defects can only be dealt with on an inter-departmental basis. Indeed TQM partly evolved from the realisation that improvements can only be achieved if professional and departmental barriers are broken down, people stop blaming each other for defects and constructively work together to solve them.
4 Valuing all staff: Because TQM emphasises each link in the internal quality chain all staff, even those traditionally seen as low status or unimportant, have a contribution to make.
5 Quality measurement is essential: 'Quality measurements for each area of activity must be established where they don't exist and reviewed where they do' (Crosby 1979: 132).
6 Corporate systems must be aligned to support TQM: Two of the great pioneers of total quality management, Edwards Deming and J.H. Juran, whose work had great influence on Japanese companies after the Second World War, discovered that quality problems were usually built into the design of production processes and could not be attributed to the ill-will or incompetence of workers. It was primarily management's responsibility to help workers to do their jobs in a high-quality way ('doing it right first time'), by identifying the sources of error and planning the production process to prevent their occurence.

7 Constant striving for improvement: TQM is a never-ending struggle to an unattainable goal. 'Improve constantly and forever the system of production and service, to improve quality and productivity and thus constantly decrease costs' (Deming 1986: 23).

The hype and fervour which surrounds TQM positively invite scepticism. However the theory behind it is sound: there is greater scope for improving performance by concentrating on the average producer than by focusing exclusively on a few 'bad apples' (Berwick 1989). Similarly there is enormous potential for reducing the cost of error and waste by redesigning the production process and achieving improvements in patient care at the same time. (For a striking example, see Box on p. 114.)

Many health authorities claim to have adopted a TQM approach to quality improvement, and the DOH funded 17 pilot sites from 1989 with more added later. However none fully meet the tenets of TQM. Criticisms made by an independent evaluation team in their interim report included:

1 The failure to carry out any organisational audit before implementing TQM to establish quality benchmarks. It was therefore difficult to tell how much progress had been made.
2 Failure to develop a corporate-wide approach to quality which would align the relevant information and management systems and processes. TQM often seemed like 'just another initiative' to be tacked on to countless others. In particular the links and potential of resource management in supporting TQM were not exploited.
3 Tensions between a corporate approach to quality like TQM with monoprofessional systems of audit and quality assurance. This was particularly apparent among the doctors, who rarely participated fully in TQM initiatives, pursuing their own system of medical audit.

Nevertheless many improvements had been made, much enthusiasm generated and a customer-focus was more apparent (Centre for the Evaluation of Public Policy and Practice 1991). The potential of TQM initiatives to empower patients is demonstrated by an example from one of the West Midlands case study districts in the 'Monitoring Managed Competition' research, who are themselves a national TQM demonstration project. The hospital had a commitment to shared care with the patient and patient's relatives and care plans were drawn up in full consultation with both. This was based on an explicit philosophy of preserving the dignity and independence of patients. The Director of Quality Assurance explained:

Far too long, for the last 40 years, you go into hospital and you lose everything. You lose control of your life. For the first time you lose control of your own fate. What we are saying is, the patient ought to be able to determine at any stage of their illness what care they receive, and they ought to know what is coming next.

The Byzantine complexity of the typical hospital[3]

To demonstrate the benefits of reorganising hospital processes along patient-centred lines, Andersen Consulting undertook a survey of 10 hospitals. The results were startling:

1 Junior doctors walked on average seven miles a day on each shift, consuming up to three hours of their productive time and adding substantially to the exhaustion they experienced. Porters were covering up to 20 miles a day.
2 A common pathology test took on average 10 people and 18 hours to carry out, and 80 per cent of all tests requested comprised a few simple procedures which could be easily carried out by nurses on the ward.
3 The typical patient came into contact with 47 care providers in the course of a five-day spell in hospital.
4 Hospitals in the survey averaged 201 job classifications.

The consultants' approach, which is being implemented in London's Central Middlesex Hospital, is to organise patient care with multiskilled teams of staff who can meet most of the patient's needs on the spot. Responsibility for planning, implementing and auditing care becomes team-based, and existing demarcation boundaries on who does what are broken down. The system is claimed to produce improved quality of care, staff morale and job satisfaction and cost savings in the order of 10–15 per cent.

Doing things to patients which they were capable of doing for themselves was also wasteful of resources:

Why should we bath someone when they are capable of bathing themselves? Why should we give their medication when they are capable of taking it themselves? Why do we need two nurses going round with a medicine tray? You take your medicine at home, why not here? If in pain control, you were in control of your own pain, you have less than if it were a set wait every four hours for us to come and give you a tablet.

Having well-informed patients who have more control over their care, and who are helped to retain independence is good for quality and is also cost-effective.

Whether it be aspirin or 10 mg. of morphine, a trained nurse has got to do both. Roughly 30 per cent of the patients in our hospital, shall we say, are just on antibiotics; they can take it themselves. That should give us at least half a whole time equivalent nurse on every ward. If you multiply that up, that is £250,000 worth of money that could then be given to alternative developments.

The Patient's Charter

Announced in a great flurry of publicity in November 1991, the Patient's Charter announced 10 'charter rights' for patients in the NHS, as part of the Citizen's Charter initiative. Seven of these simply reiterated the existing rights of NHS patients, three were new as from

---

The Patient's Charter – a summary

Seven existing rights:

1 Access to health care on the basis of clinical need, regardless of ability to pay.
2 To be registered with a GP.
3 To receive emergency medical care at any time.
4 To be referred to an acceptable consultant and have access to a second opinion, with GP agreement.
5 Informed consent to treatment.
6 Access to medical records, and assurance of their confidentiality.
7 Voluntary participation in medical training or research.

Three new rights:

8 Right to detailed information on local health services, including quality standards and maximum waiting times.
9 Guaranteed admission date for treatment within maximum time of two years from being placed on a waiting list.
10 To have all complaints investigated and to receive a full and prompt reply.

The Charter standards which the NHS aims to meet:

1 Respect for privacy, dignity and religious and cultural beliefs.
2 Arrangements to ensure everyone, including those with special needs, can use the services.
3 Relatives and friends to be kept informed about treatment, subject to patient's wishes.
4 Emergency ambulance should arrive within 14 minutes in an urban area or 19 minutes in a rural one.
5 Need for treatment assessed immediately in accident and emergency departments.
6 Specific appointment times in outpatient clinics and maximum waiting time of 30 minutes.
7 Where cancellation of operations happens twice in succession, the patient must be admitted within one month of the date of the second cancellation.
8 A named qualified nurse, midwife or health visitor responsible for each patient.
9 Planned discharge arrangements, which include provision for social care or rehabilitation needs of the patient.

April 1992. In addition nine charter standards were announced. Authorities were also asked to produce local charters which could set more ambitious and specific targets.

The Charter's public reception was qualified. While the listing and publicising of rights was welcomed (every household in the country received a copy), there was some disappointment at the unambitious nature of the targets and the absence of enforcement mechanisms. The NHS in Scotland, for example, had already set a waiting list target of 18 months compared to the two-year target adopted for England and Wales. The rhetoric of rights also contrasted oddly with the failure to give more powers to Community Health Councils, the main body representing patients locally, and cutbacks in funding Citizens' Advice Bureaus and legal aid.

Nevertheless, ministers and the NHSME took implementation seriously and kept up the pressure on Health Authorities. Extra finance was forthcoming to meet the two-year waiting list target by April 1992 and Regional Health Authorities were instructed to give its achievement high priority. Though not entirely met, ministers claimed a reduction from 50,000 to 2,000 in two-year waiters within one year. From 1992–93 the target was reduced to an 18-month maximum and many districts were aiming for a year or even less.

As the Patients' Association noted, the Charter was an important step in enabling patients to speak up for themselves as individuals outside the organisational framework of DHAs acting as 'champions of the people' and GPs as the patient's agent. The right to good quality information for patients and the public was the essential prerequisite to enable them to do so. From April 1992 DHAs and GP fundholders must ensure that:

1 Service providers give detailed information about their services and national and local charter standards to patients in an easily accessible way.
2 They themselves provide information directly through:

   - information leaflets
   - well-publicised DHA contact points and helplines (this could include 'health shops' in city centres)
   - materials for CHCs to disseminate
   - providing information to neighbourhood forums, public meetings, etc. (NHSME 1992a).

Conclusions

A mixed stew of quality initiatives bubbles throughout the NHS. This chapter has not been able to cover them all – the impetus GPFHs have had in driving through quality improvements for example (Glennerster *et al.* 1992) or the current drive to achieve the BS 5750 quality 'kitemarks'. There is no mistaking the enthusiasm which drives these initiatives and the real commitment to providing a 'user-centred' service.

Enthusiasm, however, is no substitute for conceptual clarity and agreement on objectives. What should quality mean in a public health service like the NHS? What emphasis should be given in resource terms to the sometimes competing claims of effectiveness versus 'user-friendly' services? What should the relationship with the end user be? The multiplicity of terms in current use – patient, consumer, customer – imply quite different models.

This harks back to the debate in Chapter 6 as to the transferability of concepts and systems which originate in the commercial world to the NHS without modification. Hoggett and Hambleton (1987) argue that in seeking to make public services more user-centred two approaches are discernible: consumerism which focuses on the responsiveness of public services (broadly the approach of the Major government) and collective responses which emphasise the democratisation of services.

Consumerism is a response to the critique of inward-looking public service organisations which fail to put the customer first, articulated by the *Griffiths Report* in relation to the NHS. The preferred solutions draw heavily on the lessons of the 'excellence' literature. Collectivist solutions go further than this, basing their arguments on the differences in the nature of consumption and accountability in the public and private sectors. Public managers are accountable to the public as citizens and taxpayers as well as consumers of services. Part of the social purpose of the organisation may be to enhance democratic mechanisms of accountability and diffuse participation in decision-making to wider sections of society (Hoggett and Hambleton 1987).

Finally, there is the issue of resources. Much can be achieved within present resources by doing things differently (sometimes radically so). But achieving behavioural change will require extra investment, notably in training. Who will fund this investment? Will providers be expected to within existing contracts? Will purchasing authorities be prepared to pay extra to ensure it happens?

Implementing the Patient's Charter also poses many contradictions for both parties. Apart from the inpatient waiting list initiative no extra resources were released for meeting the Charter standards, but meeting the standard for outpatient clinics may be at the expense of seeing fewer patients and a lengthening list for a first appointment. Making services accessible to those with special needs is expensive: widening entrances, building ramps, installing lifts, providing interpreting and translation services – the list is a long one.

The largesse the NHS received in an election year was predictably short-lived and the settlement for 1993 is only 0.8 per cent above the inflation forecast. The government's longer-term commitment to 'quality' public services must be in doubt as they become increasingly embattled on the economic front.

In conclusion, although it is difficult to foresee the tide of interest and activity being turned back in the NHS, and a majority of DGMs believe that the new system has already delivered quality improvements (Appleby *et al.* 1992) there is a long and contentious road to travel. The NHS has only reached the end of the beginning on the quality front.

Notes

1 Source: NAHA/NHSTA (1988).
2 Source: DOH (1989) 'Contracts for health services: operational principles', p. 17.
3 Source: Andersen Consulting 'Patient-centred care: reinventing the hospital'; see also *Financial Times* 24 June 1992.

References

Appleby, J., Little, V., Ranade, W., Robinson, R. and Smith, P. (1992) *Implementing the Reforms: A Survey of District General Managers,* Monitoring Managed Competition Project, Project paper 4, Birmingham NAHAT.

Audit Commission (1992) *The Virtue of Patients: Making Best Use of Ward Nursing Resources,* London: HMSO.

Barker, I. (1991) 'Purchasing for people', *Health Services Management,* October 187 (5): 212–14.

Berwick, D.M. (1989) 'Continuous improvement as an ideal in health care', *New England Journal of Medicine,* 320 (1): 53–56.

Black, A.D. (1986) *An Anthology of Fake Antitheses,* Rock Carling Monograph, London: Nuffield Provincial Hospitals Trust.

Brooke, R.H. and Lohr, K.N. (1988) 'Efficacy, effectiveness variations and quality: boundary crossing research', *Medical Care,* 23: 710–22.

Campling, E.A., Devlin, H.B. and Lunn, J.N. (1990) *Report of the National Confidential Enquiry into Perioperative Deaths 1989,* London: Royal College of Surgeons/Royal College of Anaesthetists.

Centre for the Evaluation of Public Policy and Practice (1991) *Evaluation of Total Quality Management Projects in the National Health Service,* Interim Report, London: Brunel University

Cook, R. (1990) *A Fresh Start for Health,* London: Labour Party.

Crosby, P. (1979) *Quality is Free,* New York: McGraw Hill.

Dalley, G. and Carr-Hill, R. (1991) *Pathways to Quality: A Study of Quality Management Initiatives in the NHS: A Guide for Managers,* York: University of York, Centre for Health Economics.

Deming, W.E. (1986) *Out of the Crisis,* Cambridge, Massachusetts: Massachusetts Institute of Technology.

Department of Health (1989) *Working for Patients – Medical Audit,* Working Paper 6, London: HMSO.

Department of Health (1990) *Contracts for Health Services: Operational principles,* p. 17, London: HMSO.

Fenwick, J. (1989) 'Consumerism and local government', *Local Government Policy-making*, 16 (1): 45–52.

Fuchs, V. (1984) 'Rationing health care', *New England Journal of Medicine*, December 18.

Glennerster, H., Matsaganis, M. and Owens, P. (1992) *A Foothold for Fundholding*, Research Report 12, London: Kings Fund Institute.

Hoggett, P. and Hambleton, R. (1987) *Decentralisation and Democracy: Localising Public Services*, Bristol: School of Advanced Urban Studies, University of Bristol.

Judge, K. and Knapp, M. (1985) 'Efficiency in the production of welfare: the public and private sectors compared' in R. Klein and M. O'Higgins (eds) *The Future of Welfare,* Oxford: Blackwell.

Koch, H. (1990) 'The changing face of the National Health Service in the 1990s', in P. Spurgeon (ed), London: Longman.

Maxwell, R. *et al.* (1983) 'Seeking quality', *Lancet* January 1/8 (8314–5): 45–8.

NAHA/NHS Training Authority (1988) *A Manual for Health Authority Chairmen and Members*, Birmingham: National Association of Health Authorities.

NHS Management Executive (1989) 'Quality', Letter to Regional and District General Managers, 22.6.1989.

——(1992a) 'Implementing the Patient's Charter' *Health Service Guidelines* HSG(92)4. January.

——(1992b) *Local Voices – The Views of Local People in Purchasing for Health*, EL(92)1. January.

Peters, T. and Austin, N. (1985) *A Passion for Excellence: the Leadership Difference*, London: Collins.

Pollitt, C. (1990) 'Capturing quality? The quality issue in British and American health policies', *Journal of Public Policy*, 7 (1): 71–92.

——(1992) 'The struggle for quality: the case of the NHS', Paper given to UK Political Studies Association Conference, Queen's University Belfast, April.

Proctor, S. (1990) 'Accountability and nursing', *Nursing Review*, 8 (3/4): 15–21.

Royal College of General Practitioners (1985) *What sort of Doctor? Assessing quality of care in general practice*, London: RCGP.

Royal College of Nursing (1989) *A Framework for Quality: A Patient-centred Approach to Quality Assurance in Health Care*, London: Royal College of Nursing.

Shaw, C.D. (undated) *Introducing Quality Assurance*, Project Paper 64, London: Kings Fund College (undated).

Wilson, J. (1992) 'The care trade: a picture of health?', Unpublished dissertation for M.Sc. Strategy and Resource Management, Newcastle Polytechnic.

Young, K. (1991) 'Consumer-centred approaches in the public/voluntary/personal services', *Public Money and Management*, Summer 11 (2): 33–9.

CHAPTER 8

Health for all?

Working for Patients was a policy document with a hole at its heart, lacking any vision or strategic direction for the NHS to take. It said a great deal about how to deliver health care, but very little about what kind of health care should be delivered. Given its neoliberal provenance and Mrs Thatcher's contempt for strategic planning and the 'nanny state' this is hardly surprising. What is more surprising is the apparent change of direction that has taken place under the Major government with the publication of the first national health strategy document, *Health of the Nation* (DOH 1992). This set targets for achieving improvements in health in five key areas and followed a year of consultation on a first draft. In addition, purchasing authorities are urged to make 'health gain' the focus for their purchasing decisions. 'Health gain' is the current jargon for achieving reductions in mortality and morbidity or improvements in quality of life; in the more memorable language of the World Health Organisation, it is 'adding years to life and life to years'.

This chapter will discuss these policies in the context of three questions: What are the principal health problems faced in Britain? What are the components of an effective national strategy for improvement? To what extent does present government policy meet these criteria?

Health and ill-health in Britain

On many measures, the health of the British population has improved greatly over the last 60 years. Life expectancy has steadily increased to 73 for males and 78 for females. Infant mortality has declined from 74 per 1,000 births in 1929 to 8.4 per 1,000 in 1989. Maternal mortality is negligible, although in the 1930s over 2,500 women died annually in childbirth. The infectious diseases of tuberculosis, poliomyelitis and diptheria have virtually been eliminated and, since the introduction of the combined measles, mumps and rubella vaccine in 1988, these diseases have declined dramatically as well.

Changes in the distribution of mortality mean that today the major causes of death are heart disease, cerebrovascular disease (stroke) and cancers, particularly lung and breast cancer. The potential seriousness of AIDS/HIV is considerable, though it is at present responsible for only a small number of deaths.

Figure 8.1 documents the changes in the distribution of total deaths from all causes by sex and age between 1931 and 1988. Figure 8.2 shows the years of life lost up to age 65. This gives more weight to deaths at younger age-groups, since a death at 15 would count as 50

Figure 8.1 **Distribution of total deaths by cause and age: 1931 and 1988**

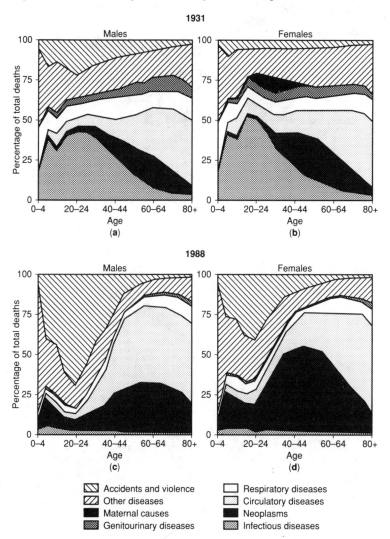

Source: Adapted from *The Health of the Nation: A Consultative document for health in England*, Cmnd. 1523, DH (1991). Crown ©. Reproduced with the permission of the controller of Her Majesty's Stationery Office.

Figure 8.2 **Distribution of years of life lost up to age 65 by cause: 1988**

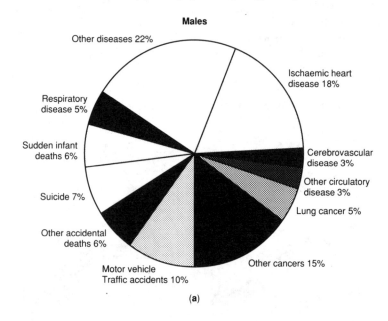

(a)

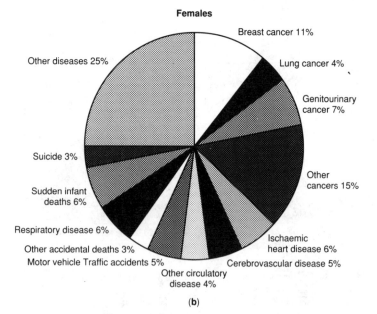

(b)

Source: Adapted from *The Health of the Nation: A Consultative document for health in England*, Cmnd. 1523, DH (1991). Crown ©. Reproduced with the permission of the controller of Her Majesty's Stationery Office.

years lost, in contrast to a death at 60 which would count as five. On this kind of analysis, deaths from accident become a more important source of years of life lost for males since it is the principal cause of mortality between the ages of 5–35. In females cancer, particularly of the breast, cervix, uterus and ovary, is a major contributor to years of life lost.

It is much more difficult to document changes in morbidity not resulting in death because of the paucity of both current and historical data. Current data sources which are typically used include reported time off work through sickness or invalidity, GP consultation rates and use made of other NHS facilities (inpatient hospital data), registration of severe visual and hearing impairment and the levels of long-standing illness as reported in the General Household Survey. Only the last two are direct measures of health. Findings from the General Household Survey are shown in Figure 8.3 below.

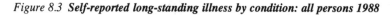

*Figure 8.3 **Self-reported long-standing illness by condition: all persons 1988***

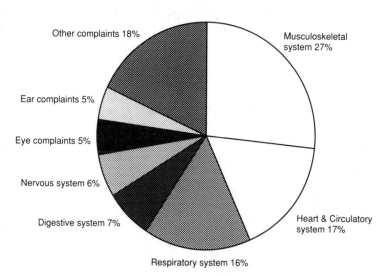

Source: Adapted from *The Health of the Nation: A Consultative document for health in England*, Cmnd. 1523, DH (1991). Crown ©. Reproduced with the permission of the controller of Her Majesty's Stationery Office.

Assessing the burden of morbidity is complicated by the different meanings attributable to 'health', and in particular the differences apparent between lay and biomedical definitions. In an important national study of the health and lifestyles of 9,000 people undertaken in 1984–85, Mildred Blaxter and her colleagues tried to capture four different dimensions of health.

1 Fitness/unfitness: this was based on physiological measurements of blood pressure, lung function and measures of height/weight by a nurse and hence represented the most objective biological measure.

2 Presence/absence of disease and impairment: medical definitions of health rest on the presence or absence of pathological symptoms, ascertained normally by clinical examination. In this study the researchers had to rely on self-report, using similar questions to the General Household Survey, for example 'Do you have any long-standing illness, disability or infirmity?' (If yes) 'What is the matter with you?' (followed by questions on the functional effects of the condition).

3 Experienced illness/freedom from illness: many people underreport symptoms of disease and impairment, either because they dismiss their significance or because they are undiagnosed and untreated. The researchers tested for this by asking respondents if they had experienced 16 common illness symptoms ranging from back pain to headaches 'in the past month'.

4 Psychosocial malaise or well-being: this was tested by asking questions on the experience of depression, worry, stress, feelings of strain, and so forth.

Unfortunately it is not possible to do justice here to the rich and fascinating data produced by the survey, and the intriguing patterns which occur on scores for the four dimensions of health by social group. The authors do, however, try to produce a summary index score on all four dimensions which distinguishes between different health categories. The results are shown by age-group and sex in Table 8.1. Table 8.2 shows the proportion taking prescribed drugs in the three major health categories.

Table 8.1 **Distribution of combined health categories by age and gender (per cent)**

| | 8.1(a) | *Males* | | | |
| | | *Age* | | | |
Health category	*18–29*	*30–44*	*45–59*	*60–69*	*70+*
Excellent	19	11	5	4	2
Good	34	33	23	18	16
Good but unfit	7	11	17	16	18
Good but poor psycho-social health	14	10	7	3	3
High illness without disease	7	9	7	7	8
'Silent' disease*	7	9	15	15	12
Poor, non-limiting disease	5	8	10	13	16
Very poor, limiting disease	6	7	17	23	24
(N=100%)	(738)	(986)	(72)	(452)	(361)

Health category	8.1(b)	*Females* *Age* *18–29*	*30–44*	*45–59*	*60–69*	*70+*
Excellent		10	9	5	3	3
Good		31	31	20	15	10
Good but unfit		6	8	10	14	13
Good but poor psycho-social health		21	14	10	8	4
High illness without disease		17	13	14	12	12
'Silent' disease*		4	6	6	9	8
Poor, non-limiting disease		6	9	14	17	18
Very poor, limiting disease		5	9	18	23	32
(N=100%)		(879)	(1,318)	(926)	(562)	(414)

Note: 'Silent' disease refers to a disease without any functional consequences or high rate of illness symptoms. This included some people with sight or hearing problems, skin disease, or orthopaedic problems which did not impair mobility.
Source: Blaxter (1990) *Health and Lifestyles*, Routledge.

Table 8.2 **Proportions taking prescribed drugs in different health categories (per cent)**

Health category	*Males* *Age* *18–39*	*40–59*	*60+*	*Females* *18–39*	*40–59*	*60+*
Excellent	2	7	19	9	9	29
Good	5	12	26	14	18	23
Very poor	42	73	87	58	74	88

Source: Blaxter (1990) *Health and Lifestyles*, Routledge.

Aggregate figures conceal large variations in the health experience of different groups. Age, gender, ethnic and socio-economic status, occupation, place of residence: all affect objective and subjective measures of health in ways which are not completely understood. Mortality rates from coronary heart disease, for example, which accounts for 26 per cent of all deaths, vary considerably within each country and region of the United Kingdom, with Scotland and Northern Ireland having the dubious distinction of heading the world league table (see Table 8.3 and Figure 8.4).

Table 8.3 **Standardised mortality ratios for coronary heart disease for men and women in the standard UK regions in 1985 (all ages)**

	Men*	Women*
Scotland	119	123
Northern Ireland	118	123
North West	117	116
North	116	124
Yorkshire and Humberside	111	116
Wales	111	106
West Midlands	103	104
East Midlands	99	102
South West	91	88
South East	89	87
East Anglia	86	89

* all UK = 100

Source: Newcastle DHA, *CHD Prevention Policy,* 3 November 1988.
Crown ©. Reproduced with the permission of the controller of Her Majesty's Stationery Office.

Regional figures disguise even more marked local differences. Figures for the 'best' and 'worst' districts in the Northern region are shown in Table 8.4, together with figures for the 'best' and 'worst' local authority wards in one Northern city, Newcastle upon Tyne.

Table 8.4 **Standardised mortality ratios for coronary heart disease for men and women – 'best' and 'worst' districts in the Northern Region, (Deaths under 65, 1984–86) and 'best' and 'worst' wards in Newcastle upon Tyne (Deaths under 65, 1981–86)**

	Men	Women
Northern Region	124	138
South Cumbria (best district)	100	107
N.W. Durham (worst district)	147	188
Newcastle upon Tyne	124	133
South Gosforth (best ward)	78	67
Monkchester (worst ward)	189	250
All UK	100	100

Source: Newcastle DHA, Public Health Report 1990

The most striking and shocking fact that emerges from these figures is that within a radius of barely three miles in one city the risk of dying

Figure 8.4 *Coronary heart disease mortality rates for men and women aged 40–69 – international comparisons 1985*

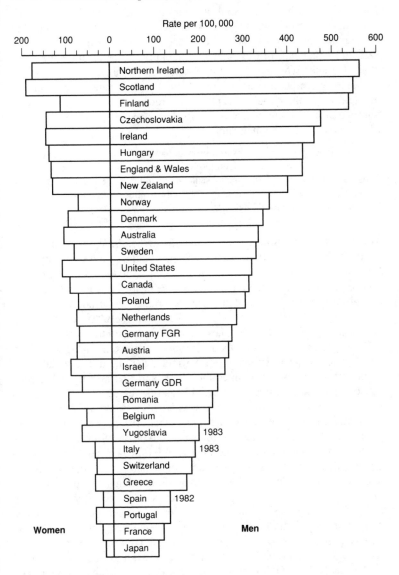

Source: Newcastle DHA, *CHD Prevention Policy*, 3 November 1988.
Crown ©. Reproduced with the permission of the controller of Her Majesty's Stationery Office.

from coronary heart disease is over three times higher for men, and four times higher for women. Unsurprisingly, South Gosforth is one of the wealthiest wards in the city, Monkchester one of the poorest.

Health inequalities and social class – the evidence

The association between social position and health status is one of the best documented findings in social science, and Britain has a long and honourable tradition of such research, going back to the enquiries of Farr and Chadwick in the nineteenth century. More recently the work of the Black Working Party on social class inequalities in health triggered enormous research interest among the academic community in spite of the cool reception it received from government. Summarising the evidence of a further decade of work in 1987 Margaret Whitehead concluded:

Whether social position is measured by occupational class, or by assets such as house and car-ownership, or by employment status, a similar picture emerges. Those at the bottom of the social scale have much higher death rates than those at the top. This applies at every stage of life from birth, through to adulthood and well into old age.

(Whitehead 1987: 1)

This was true for almost every indicator of health status: death rates from all the major killer diseases, chronic sickness and disability, low birth weight, height and weight of children. Blaxter's work confirms this picture. On all four dimensions of health in the study and at each age group 'there was a tendency for experience to be poorer as social class declined' (Blaxter 1990: 66). The gap between manual and nonmanual groups was particularly marked in the middle years of life.

Research on health and inequality has provoked much academic debate and political dissension, in particular the claim that social class inequalities have widened since the 1950s and that poverty is the root cause rather than cultural or personal life-style factors.

The claim that health inequalities widened between 1951 and 1972, originally made in the *Black Report* (Black 1980), was subject to a good deal of methodological criticism (Wilkinson 1986; Illsley 1986; Illsley and Le Grand 1987; see also Klein 1988). In particular it was argued that the changing size and composition of classes made historical comparisons problematic, or the findings could be due to differential social mobility (poor health causes low social status, rather than the reverse). Since then a number of important studies have painstakingly tried to overcome these difficulties with results that largely reinforce the *Black Report's* findings (Townsend 1990a, 1990b; see also Whitehead 1987, Wilkinson 1989). Marmot and McDowall's (1986) analysis of Office of Population Census and Surveys data over the period 1979–1983 confirms a continuing widening trend into the 1980s (see Table 8.5).

It is important to be clear about what is being asserted. All social classes have enjoyed substantial improvements in health over time but

Table 8.5 **Trends in male mortality by class, 1970–83 England and Wales**

		Age-standardised mortality rates (per 1,000)		
Occupational Class		1970–72 (ages 15–64)	1979–80 and 1982–83 (ages 20–64)	Percentage improvement
I	Professional	4.62	3.71	+20
II	Senior admin/ managerial	4.86	4.18	+14
III	Skilled non manual	5.91	5.21	+12
IV	Partly skilled manual	6.81	6.41	+6
V	Unskilled manual	8.32	9.09	−9
	All	5.97	5.43	+9

Source: Newcastle DHA, *CHD prevention policy*, 3 November 1988.
Crown ©. Reproduced with the permission of the controller of Her Majesty's Stationery Office.

those improvements have been faster in the more prosperous social classes than in the poorer ones. Similarly, improvements in death rates in infancy and childhood have 'bunched' the majority of deaths into later middle and old age, and this is true for all social classes, but deaths at those ages are still highly unequal.

Since 1979, Conservative governments have a sorry record of trying to dismiss or suppress evidence of widening health inequalities, which borders at times on the ludicrous (Thunhurst 1991). Where the evidence is incontrovertible, the second line of attack is to dispute the primary cause. The *Black Report* attributed the worse health records of the lower social classes to lower incomes, poorer working and living conditions, higher exposure to risk and insecurity; in other words the material conditions of life they experience which are socially and economically structured. An alternative explanation, largely reflected in government policy, puts more emphasis on the life-styles and health choices that individuals make. The poorer social classes smoke and drink more, eat less healthy diets, take less exercise and appear to put less value on future health as assessed for example by the take-up of preventive health care.

In a major study of health inequalities in 678 local authority wards in the Northern region, Townsend and his colleagues (Townsend *et al.* 1987) took the argument further by trying to relate health status to direct measures of material deprivation. Health status was assessed by three measures combined into a single index: standardised mortality, percentage of low birth weight babies, percentage of chronically ill and disabled. The four indicators of material deprivation were percentage unemployed, house and car ownership and household overcrowding.

The results largely supported the *Black Report*'s conclusions, with material deprivation accounting for 65 per cent of the variance in health status between wards. In spite of this impressive evidence, Edwina Currie, then Junior Health Minister, visiting the Northern region on the day the report was released, commented: 'I honestly don't think (health) has anything to do with poverty. The problem very often for many people is just ignorance . . . and failing to realise they do have some control over their own lives' (quoted in Townsend 1990b: 383).

This of course is the central point, the extent to which people *do* have control over the forces which shape their lives and are capable of making the changes necessary for a healthier life-style. One well-founded theory of behavioural change asserts that if people believe they can achieve what they want through their own actions (internal locus of control) they are more likely to change their attitudes and behaviour in the desired directions. If people believe their lives are shaped by forces beyond their control (external locus of control) there is less incentive to make changes. But these attitudes and perceptions are influenced and shaped by material circumstances as well as cultural beliefs. As Graham points out in her discussion of family health:

Health choices are shaped by material as well as mental structures. The barriers to change are represented by the limits of time, energy and income available to parents. In such circumstances health choices are more accurately seen as health compromises, which, repeated day after day, become the routines which keep the family going.

(Graham 1984: 94)

Choosing a healthy diet

A brief look at some of the evidence on dietary patterns illustrates Graham's point. Basic knowledge about what constitutes a 'healthy' diet is now fairly widespread, through government health education messages, women's magazines and food advertising. Several studies have shown that even low income groups are well-informed about the need for more fruit and fresh vegetables in the diet, more fibre and less fat (Jones 1992, MacDonald and Hanes 1988; HEA 1989) and express a desire to eat more of these foods if they could afford them. Income is also not a barrier to healthy food choices over a broad range of incomes (Wilson 1987, Blaxter 1990), the exceptions being low income families and families where men keep tight control over patterns of spending, including food expenditure. Blaxter concluded that income, education and region were the best predictors of a healthy diet, with education having the strongest effect except for women between the ages of 40–59 where income remained the most important variable (pp. 125–126).

In low income families the constraints on healthy diets are severe. At Income Support levels families would need to spend 50 per cent of their incomes on food to attain the nutritional standards recommended by the government's advisory body (NACNE 1983, MacDonald and Hanes 1988). A recent research report on diet among low income mothers in the North East shows that in practice many are spending this proportion of their income on food, leaving very little for all the other necessities of life (Jones 1992). The 62 women in the sample all had at least one child under five. Average gross household incomes ranged from £60 to £100 per week, and 71 per cent spent more than 30 per cent of their income on food, with one in five spending more than 50%. Analysis of food diaries kept by the women showed that, in spite of this, diets were seriously imbalanced, high in fat and low in fibre, and provided lower than the total energy requirements recommended by the government. There were serious deficiencies of many vitamins and essential minerals through shortages of fresh vegetables and fruit. The availability of 'healthy' foods like wholemeal bread, low fat spreads and semiskimmed milk locally was limited and even when available the price difference with less healthy alternatives – whole milk, white bread and economy margarines – was greater than in more affluent areas of the city.

Menus were also affected by the availability of facilities for food preparation and storage. As income increased so did facilities, and the preparation and cooking of food from raw materials, although cooking skills generally were poorer in the younger age groups. There was another logic to the greater use of convenience foods by the poorest women however which was that they eliminated waste, rendering precise measurement possible. 'Junk' foods are also a cheaper source of calories: according to the London Food Survey they are cheaper than the cheapest form of healthy diet (Lang and Cole-Hamilton 1986).

Wilson argues that poverty reinforces conservative food choices, since women cannot afford to experiment with foods which husbands or children may reject. Indeed the food preferences of the family are a major constraint in changing towards healthier diets across all income levels as long as the preparation and serving of food is so intimately bound up with the gendered nature of the marriage contract and the association of food with love and comfort. For this reason, women often cook separate things for different members of the family, and in general are turning more to convenience foods to save work, particularly when cooking for children (Wilson 1989).

In terms of gender differences, women eat less and have healthier food preferences than men (Whichelow 1987, Newby 1983, Wilson 1987), although this is also affected by education. Large appetites and 'proper meals' which contained meat appear to be part of the construction of masculinity among some social groups (the 'real men don't eat quiche' syndrome). To sum up, the evidence suggests that health education messages about healthy diets have been fairly successful: most people know what they should do to eat well, but cultural and structural constraints prevent them from doing so. Low income is the most severe barrier of all. As Wilson points out health education is simply irrelevant as a guide to action in poor families.

> In these households it is more important to avoid waste than to try and convert an overstressed family to foods it does not know. Health education has to be seen as an investment for better times. Its immediate effect can only be to increase worry rather than lead to action.
>
> (Wilson 1989: 183)

Income and not ignorance is the main determinant of the diet of low income families (although education, culture and gender relations within the family also exert their effects), hence policies to increase their incomes (particularly the resources that women control like child benefit) or their access to healthy food (for example, take-up of nutritionally sound school meals) should be given priority.

The evidence also suggests that health education efforts could more profitably be targeted on men rather than women since men's food habits are less healthy, and the assumption that women can determine what other members of the family eat is only partly true.

Finally, the evidence shows the growing reliance of all income groups on processed and semiprocessed foods, and hence on the policies of the agricultural, food processing and retail distribution industries and the government departments which regulate them. The food scares of recent years – salmonella in eggs, listeria in cheese, 'mad cow disease' through infected animal feed – demonstrates how little control individuals have over the safety and quality of food that appears in the shops as a result of the production methods of agribusiness. In addition health education messages from the DOH are contradicted by the policies of other departments. Until the late 1980s the Milk Marketing Board ensured that only full-fat milk appeared on our doorsteps in an effort not to increase the European butter mountain by skimming the fat off (Robbins 1991). Through the illogic of the Common Agricultural Policy (CAP) farmers received a premium on producing full-fat milk, and the growing of sugar beet and even tobacco is still subsidised under CAP. Policies to ensure a healthier British diet would have to tackle these issues as well as a raft of others: food labelling, the link between additives and allergies or other illnesses, the targeting of 'unhealthy' products at children, the pricing and distribution policies of the retail chains. Individuals do have choices to make but within the context set by government and industry who can either make the healthy choice the easy choice or not.

A strategy for health – Health for All 2000

A successful strategy for health must tackle its socio-economic and environmental determinants and replace the existing dominant 'medical' model of health with a social model. The World Health Organisation's (WHO) 'Health for All 2000' (HFA) has been particularly influential and some of its policy off-shoots, notably Healthy Cities and the concept of 'healthy public policy', have excited imagination and inspired national and local action in many countries.

Central to the development of HFA has been the emergence of what has become known as the New Public Health. Ashton dates its birth to McKeown's work in the early 1970s and the sociological and feminist attack on medicine discussed in Chapter Two (Ashton and Seymour 1988). In policy terms its beginnings are often traced to the *Lalonde Report* produced by the Canadian federal health minister, Marc Lalonde in 1974. The report argued along McKeown lines that further improvements in the health of Canadians depended far more on environmental and life-style change than on improvements in health care and medical science.

The *Lalonde Report* triggered renewed interest in public health and prevention in many other countries, coinciding as it did with growing disillusion about the costs and limits of therapeutic medicine. This growing momentum found expression in WHO's Global Strategy for Health for All by the Year 2000 (WHO 1981). At its Thirtieth World Health Assembly the organisation resolved in May 1977 that: 'the main social target of governments and WHO in the coming decades should be the attainment by all citizens of the world by the year 2000 of a level of health that will permit them to lead a socially and economically productive life'. At the Alma-Ata Conference in the Soviet Union the following year the organisation committed itself to primary health care as the key to achieving this goal (WHO 1985).

The European Regional Committee of WHO then produced a regional strategy for health as the framework for accomplishing HFA which was adopted by all 32 member states in 1980. The strategy was developed into 38 targets which specified the maximum progress European countries should make in improving health, and this too was endorsed by all the members (WHO 1985).

Six major themes underlie the targets and the whole HFA strategy, which is also based on the definition of health adopted by WHO as 'a state of complete physical, social and mental well-being and not merely the absence of disease or infirmity'(WHO 1946). The themes are:

1 Equity in health: Present inequalities in health between countries and within countries should be reduced as far as possible.
2 Health promotion and prevention of disease: The aim is to develop health in the positive sense of a resource for life, so that people can

make best use of their capacities. The emphasis should therefore be on health promotion and prevention of disease.

3 Community participation: Health for all can only be attained with the active participation of the whole community. This means giving people the skills and knowledge to empower them to take control of their own health, and implies a different relationship between professional workers and the community – summed up by the phrase 'professionals on tap, not on top'.

4 Multisectoral cooperation: The multidimensional determinants of health require cooperation between government, business, academia, voluntary and community organisations.

5 Primary health care: The focus of the health care system should be on meeting basic health needs of the community as fully as possible through easily accessible primary health care services.

6 International cooperation: Many health problems transcend national frontiers, for example AIDS, pollution, traffic in health-damaging goods, and solutions require international cooperation.

The concept of health promotion

Health promotion was the backbone of the new public health and a key concept in the strategy of health for all. Tannahill (1987) defines it as encompassing three overlapping types of activity: health education, prevention and health protection. The first two can be seen as the more traditional roles of the health promoter but activities which fall under the rubric of health protection extend the remit more widely to include advocacy and campaigning for policy change in all spheres affecting health (what David Player, former Director of the Health Education Authority, has termed 'trouble making for health').

In the context of HFA, the Ottawa Charter of Health Promotion in 1986 (WHO 1986) fleshed out the concept and potential for action as:

1 Building healthy public policy;
2 Creating supportive environments;
3 Strengthening community action;
4 Developing personal skills;
5 Reorienting health services.

All are interlinked. Building healthy public policy involves putting health on the agenda of public policy-makers in all sectors and at all levels, identifying barriers to health-promoting policies and ways of removing them. Creating supportive environments means developing the social and physical environments which establish the conditions for health and healthy behaviour, and accepting as a guiding principle of social life 'reciprocal maintenance – to take care of each other, our communities and our natural environment' (WHO 1986). Strengthening the capacity for community action means developing social networks and support systems, and helping people develop the skills and knowledge they need to take greater control of their own health. (Figure 8.5 shows the ways of doing this at the local level.)

Figure 8.5 **Community action for health at city level**

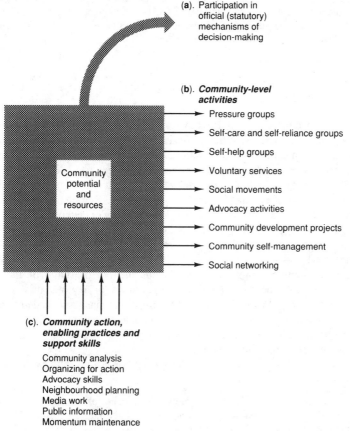

(a). Participation in official (statutory) mechanisms of decision-making

(b). **Community-level activities**

Pressure groups

Self-care and self-reliance groups

Self-help groups

Voluntary services

Social movements

Advocacy activities

Community development projects

Community self-management

Social networking

Community potential and resources

(c). **Community action, enabling practices and support skills**

Community analysis
Organizing for action
Advocacy skills
Neighbourhood planning
Media work
Public information
Momentum maintenance

Source: Adapted, by permission, from Tsouros, A. (ed) *WHO Healthy Cities Project: A project becomes a movement*, Copenhagen, WHO Regional office for Europe, 1991.

Reorienting health services means moving beyond the traditional provision of curative and clinical services. Recognising that most of the causes of ill-health lie outside the direct influence of the medical sector, health professionals must be willing to work with those who can influence those causes.

The new public health therefore is challenged to move radically beyond its old frontiers and develop renewed links with social justice, social change and reform. It is also closely linked with the Green movement: societies that pollute and destroy their natural environment reap a bitter harvest of sickness and disease. Kickbusch offers the following working definition of the new public health which encompasses these ideas:

Public health is the science and art of promoting health. It does so on the understanding that health is a process engaging social, mental, spiritual and physical well-being. It bases its actions on the knowledge that health is a fundamental resource to the individual, the community and to society as a whole and must be supported through sound investments into conditions of living that create, maintain and protect health.

(Kickbusch 1989)

Charting progress

What achievements does HFA have to its credit? Altenstetter (1989) argues that its successes lie more in changing political and social attitudes to health, and internationalising the debate, than in the achievement of health outcomes, although progress has been made on some of the targets. Each member state is required to monitor and report progress at regular intervals and the HFA Regional Office for Europe has done much good work clarifying concepts and the indicators to be used. This has led to considerable improvements in the routine information available for monitoring health trends on a comparative basis, exposing political and professional elites in many countries to unfavourable evidence about the health status of their populations and the fact that for some groups or regions this was declining. The World Health Organisation has succeeded in internationalising the terms of the health debate among policy planners and health experts and there is now widespread acceptance of the basic philosophy and tenets underpinning HFA.

In concrete terms it has led to the reorientation of health policy in many countries. By 1988:

18 countries either have finished or are in the process of making their own national HFA policy, following the framework of the target document; four finished this process during the last 12 months, five have started the process, and the other nine all made major advances in their work. The remaining countries are those where prevailing conditions were more difficult, e.g. countries with more federal structure and weaker planning mandates, or countries where pressure groups were initially sceptical. . . . By now there seems no longer to be an organised resistance to the application of the European HFA targets in any country in Europe.

(WHO 1988)

A paradigm shift of this scale is a very real achievement but the gulf between understanding and action remains a chasm: 'The political failure to introduce or sustain an explicit health concern into policy-making systems at all levels of decision making and implementation can be observed fairly widely in Europe' (Altenstetter 1989: 25).

Think globally, act locally – the Healthy Cities movement

The Healthy Cities movement has provided an important test bed and learning network for implementing HFA at the local level. The idea was born in 1984 at a conference in Toronto, still at the forefront of the new public health 10 years after Lalonde, and with a mission to become 'the healthiest city in the world by the year 2000'. One paper at the conference (Duhl 1986) argued that cities might provide the focus for an ecological and holistic approach to health in accordance with the HFA principles and strategy.

The project itself started in 1985. The original intention was for WHO to work with a small number of cities to develop ways of giving practical expression to HFA principles and to develop innovative examples of the new health promotion in practice, developing models from which others could learn. Cities were an appropriate level to test out the concepts. Although responsibilities vary in each country, most cities administer a large number of services that impact on health, and possess their own political mandate and sense of civic identity. In addition over 75 per cent of Europeans and a majority of the world's people will live in cities or large towns by the year 2000. Cities are often very unhealthy places to live, particularly for the poor, just as their nineteenth century predecessors were. It was fitting that the new public health blazed a trail in the cities just as the old public health based on the sanitary revolution did before it.

WHO's Healthy City planning group which first met in 1986 initially intended a modest project involving five to eight cities. This was quickly enlarged to accommodate the enormous interest shown in the project which mushroomed in four years to incorporate 30 project cities in 18 European countries, 17 national networks and three international networks to encompass over four hundred cities and towns in Europe, North America and Australia. The project is rapidly becoming a global movement as cities in the developing world become involved as well. More debatable is the extension of the concept to small towns and communities within cities, since although they can work to the same principles they do not have the same political and policy scope.

But what is a healthy city? Creating a vision of what people dream their city could become is the first step on the road. The Toronto City Department of Public Health pioneered the idea of vision workshops in which groups of people try to create a shared vision of what they would like their city to be. The process has been repeated in many cities since (Hancock 1988). In terms of broad categories there seems to be widespread agreement on what a healthy city would look like though in emphasis each city is unique. For example, Hancock argues that, most unusually, the quality of the physical environment was hardly mentioned in the vision workshops conducted in Canberra, the capital of Australia, simply because an exceptionally good physical environment had already been achieved. Instead participants put strong emphasis on the need for stronger social networks and stronger local democracy in a city that lacked its own tier of elected local government.

The qualities of a healthy city

A healthy city should strive to provide all its citizens with:

1 A clean, safe environment of high quality;
2 A way of life that does not destroy the natural environment or exhaust it of irreplaceable resources;
3 A strong supportive community;
4 The opportunity to influence and control decisions that affect their lives;
5 The basic needs of life: food, water, health, shelter, safety and self-respect;
6 A wide range of opportunities to experience life to the full and know and meet with other citizens;
7 An economy that provides a full range of work opportunities;
8 The opportunity to value the history and heritage of their city;
9 A form and an organisation which allow and encourage all the previous points;
10 Optimum level of health care;
11 Good mental and physical health and low levels of disease.

The project cities undertook:

1 To make health issues and the strategy of health for all more visible at the local level;
2 To move health high on the political and social agenda of the city and develop healthy public policies at the municipal level;
3 To change the way organisations and agencies work in order to encourage cooperation between departments and sectors, and strengthen community action;
4 To create innovative action for health that emphasises the interaction between people, environments, life-styles and health. Inevitably the priorities and entry points for action would depend on the cities' social and economic status and priorities from major environmental actions to programmes to support individual life-style change.

In trying to meet these challenges, participants have developed a wealth of innovatory initiatives, of which only a flavour can be given here.

1 Action for equity:
   ● providing information or targeting services on disadvantaged or underserved groups;

- community development work in small areas;
- focusing environmental improvements on the areas worst affected (in Padua this encompassed mapping noise levels, dealing with traffic, improving mobility through the creation of bicycle and walkways, dealing with solid waste disposal and researching levels of air pollution).

2 Creating supportive environments:
- greening and cleaning the city (children in Barcelona and Liverpool greened derelict areas with the help of professional gardeners according to their own design; citizens in Liege took direct action to clean their streets);
- ecological planning of new districts, or action to restore ecological balance in old ones;
- introduction of more environmentally friendly transport systems;
- using major events to take action on a broad front (for example, the decision to make the Barcelona Olympics completely non-smoking, and to support a city-wide fitness programme);
- providing information in innovative ways (Rennes has a sophisticated telecommunications project which utilises ordinary telephone lines providing a wide range of information to every household).

3 Action for community involvement:
- setting up new mechanisms for formally involving the community in urban planning and decision-making;
- facilitating community control in the design of new housing estates;
- supporting integrated community housing and economic regeneration initiatives;
- decentralising services;
- involving children in improving their neighbourhoods.

4 Action for healthy public policy:
- creating city wide networks to plan policy and strategy on specific issues, such as services for the disabled, crime or accident prevention;
- mapping environmental pollution.

5 Reorienting health services:
- developing primary care services;
- multisectoral nutrition policies and action;
- research on self-care practices;
- resourcing self-help groups.

These examples only relate to the 30 project cities; many more equally innovative developments took place under the HFA banner in hundreds more cities.

Reviewing progress made between 1987 and 1990, Tsouros (1991) usefully charts the main difficulties and problems the project cities faced and how they sought to resolve them. Developing new styles of action is one of the most challenging. The new health promotion cuts across traditional departmental and agency boundaries and HFA requires new partnerships and coalitions for health, between the powerful and powerless, in surprising and unexpected combinations.

In the long term, this requires nothing less than a fundamental change in the culture and management of city government which models very closely the trends in organisation and management discussed in earlier chapters. Influence and negotiation become more important than directives and control; power-sharing replaces power-wielding; collegial structures that support collaboration replace functional hierarchies. The styles, strategies and values that support effective health promotion are consistent with some of the megatrends of the information age.

The road to Utopia?

'Where there is no vision, the people perish' (Proverbs 29: 18)

Many of the targets of HFA were impossibly ambitious, perhaps unreachable, and to some extent the mere fact of setting quantitative targets made it a sitting duck for sceptics. But the importance of HFA and Healthy Cities lies in the process not just the goals. WHO states that the main aim of Healthy Cities was 'to change how individuals, communities, private and voluntary organisations and local governments throughout Europe think about, understand and make decisions about health' (Tsouros 1991: 39). This is an exercise in the long-term management of fundamental social change. The exercise has succeeded in inspiring many thousands of public and political activists and ordinary people with an alternative social vision based squarely on the values of participation, equity, sustainable development and cooperation. At the heart of the vision is an enriched understanding of health, not as 'complete well-being' which is both a static and utopian concept but as 'wholeness' in individuals and societies.

It is hard to hold on to the vision in the midst of severe recession, when civil wars devastate the heart of Europe, inequalities both within and between countries worsen and the environmental promises of governments seep away under the impact of economic crisis. Even its most convinced supporters have to admit that 'battling for the new public health can seem like taking on the world' (Draper and Harrison 1991: 257). Yet the vision and the values which underpin it seem to have increasing urgency and relevance when old solutions and dogmas signally fail to address the environmental, social and economic threats that the world faces. It is a vision which can inspire us with new hope.

Constraints and opportunities: the British perspective

The British government has not been at the forefront of the new public health. WHO requires each member state to evaluate its progress on meeting HFA goals and targets at periodic intervals. The 1985 British report was marked by complacency and self-satisfaction (Dooris 1987) Britain resisted translating HFA into a meaningful national policy and strategy, and its report is highly selective ignoring the issues of community participation, equity and intersectoral working and focusing entirely on the role of the NHS. By contrast HFA stimulated a good deal of activity and interest from other organisations at national and local level. By the late 1980s the Healthy Cities movement in particular had stimulated many local and health authorities into action, and its combination of vision and pragmatism had great appeal. But the prospects for local action were constrained by the government's lack of political commitment to, or even understanding of, HFA's principles and prerequisites. Indeed the thrust of public policy and the ideology of Thatcherism were antithetical to these principles: growing centralisation, sustained attacks on the autonomy and powers of local government, the subordination of social goals for macro-economic ones and the disparagement of collective values created a hostile environment.

The NHS reforms, however, created a new opportunity for public health through the separation of purchasing and providing functions, and the new strategic role given to health authorities. It was NHS managers and professionals themselves who seized the opportunity of shaping that role in a public health direction and influencing the direction of policy, in the working parties established by the NHSME after the White Paper's publication.

Health authorities had already been required to appoint Directors of Public Health following the recommendations of the *Acheson Report* (DOH 1988) in 1989 and to produce annual reports on the local population's health. These started appearing in 1990 and are already proving an important focus in some areas for local debates on priorities. Over a period of years they should lead to more incisive and systematic analyses and indicators of health and illness which inform local and regional purchasing strategies and more sharply focused contracts.

In their new role, visionary health authorities, acting within an HFA framework, could lead and coordinate imaginative strategies for health and act as catalysts for change. For example, a district strategy for childhood accidents will still require the purchase of NHS services for treatment and rehabilitation, but accident prevention lies largely outside the NHS. Health authorities can lead, coordinate and support change but most of the action takes place elsewhere. For example, they could fund a local group organising the loan of home safety equipment or installation of smoke detectors to poor families whose needs are identified by health visitors. They may coordinate an alliance of groups commited to road accident prevention which would involve among others the police, traffic and transport planners, schools, hospital accident and emergency departments and local groups of parents to share information, agree targets, and implement plans and programmes. These may range from rerouting traffic and expanding pedestrianisation in the city; traffic calming schemes in estates; planning accident-free routes to schools; the extension of bicycle paths; coordinated action against joy-riding, and so on. As advocates for health, they could campaign for more effective safety regulation on play equipment, or the wearing of bicycle helmets.

Imaginative strategies of this kind related to health gain could start to transform the NHS into a health service for the first time in its history. Another important stimulus to this development is the publication of the White Paper, *Health of the Nation* (DOH 1992), the first real attempt to adopt a national strategy for health.

Health of the nation: a new direction?

In April 1991 John Major called his cabinet to a seminar on health with a number of health experts. The outcome was a consultative document on a national health strategy in June 1991. The paper (DOH 1991) discussed a number of key areas which could be selected as national health priorities. The criteria for selection were threefold:

1   It should be a major cause of premature death or avoidable ill-health;
2   Effective interventions are possible, offering significant scope for improvement;
3   It should be possible to set quantified targets for improvement and monitor progress through specific indicators.

Sixteen possible candidates for inclusion were then discussed. The document was seen as a considerable step forward for several reasons. It gave firm support to the importance of health promotion as a central part of the 'mission' of the NHS, there was greater acknowledgement of the multidimensional determinants of health, and the Department planned to put in place some of the essential research and monitoring arrangements to support a health strategy. But the document, though acknowledging its debt to WHO's HFA strategy and targets, fell far short of its principles. There is no serious discussion of health inequalities and their causes. Equity in health, the centrepiece of HFA, is banished to a bald comment in an Appendix:

There is a persistent gap between death rates among manual and non-manual classes, and the Regional Target of reducing the actual differences in health status between groups within countries by at least 25 per cent by the year 2000 does not seem likely on present evidence to be achieved, at least with respect to those social groups.

(DOH 1991: 105)

In emphasis, life-style change by individuals still took precedence over concerted policy change by government. There is little detail on how an integrated government health strategy can be delivered, or how the long-term commitment of other departments (including the Treasury) could be ensured. In addition many health authorities were worried about how performance would be assessed. Were they to be held responsible for health outcomes over which they had limited control?

The consultation period produced an enormous response, with over 2,000 organisations and individuals responding (DOH 1992), dozens of conferences and seminars. But enthusiasm within the Cabinet seems to have waned in that time and the new Health Secretary, Virginia Bottomley, had difficulty in pushing her White Paper through. Once again, it seems to have been pressure from the top of the NHSME and the Chief Medical Officer, Kenneth Calman, which helped to tip the balance. Significantly the price for acceptance was her agreement to drop the DOH's support for a ban on tobacco advertising, a poor augury for the success of the new health strategy (*Health Service Journal* 1992).

The White Paper appeared in July 1992. Five initial priority areas which met the criteria for selection out of the 16 originally discussed were chosen, and sharper implementation arrangements were identified. A Ministerial Cabinet committee covering 11 government departments was established to oversee the implementation of the English strategy and coordinate UK-wide health policy issues. Three top-level Departmental Working Groups, originally set up when the consultative document was published, will continue to plan the implementation of particular aspects of the strategy in England (the Scottish and Welsh Office are responsible for the arrangements for Scotland and Wales).

The White Paper discusses the role of local authorities, voluntary sector, Health Education Authority, media and others in the strategy. Support for Healthy Cities is promised, indeed the government's enthusiasm for healthy environments seems to know no bounds: the paper talks of promoting 'healthy workplaces', 'healthy hospitals', 'healthy schools', 'healthy homes', even 'healthy prisons'!

On more familiar ground the White Paper spells out in detail the role and responsibilities of the NHS in implementing the strategy and the organisational arrangements the Department is putting in place. The key areas and targets are to be the core for the overall objectives of the NHS: 'Increasingly NHS authorities' performance will be measured against the efficient use of resources and working with others, to achieve improvements in the health of the people' (DOH 1992: 34). Coordinators will be appointed to lead at regional level, and RHAs will set targets and goals for DHAs and FHSAs monitored through the annual performance review process.

Finally, a strengthened information and research capability at central and regional level is an essential component of the strategy. Expanded

---

Health of the Nation – a summary of key areas and main targets:

1 Coronary heart disease and stroke – by the year 2000
 - to reduce deaths from CHD in under-65s by at least 40 per cent;
 - to reduce deaths from CHD in 65–74s by at least 30 per cent and deaths from stroke by 40 per cent.

2 Cancer – by the year 2000
 - to reduce deaths from breast cancer in the screened population by at least 25 per cent *;
 - to reduce cervical cancer by at least 20 per cent;
 - to reduce deaths from lung cancer in under-75s by at least 30 per cent in men and 15 per cent in women;
 - to halt deaths from skin cancer by the year 2005.

3 Mentally ill people – to improve significantly the health of mentally ill people and by the year 2000
 - to reduce suicides by at least 15 per cent;
 - to reduce suicides among severely mentally ill people by at least 33 per cent.

4 HIV/AIDS and sexual health
 - to reduce gonorrhoea by at least 20 per cent by 1995;
 - to reduce conceptions by under-16s by at least 50 per cent by 2000**.

5 Accidents – by the year 2005
 - to reduce deaths from accident among children under 15 by at at least 33 per cent;
 - to reduce accidental deaths among 15–24s by at least 25 per cent; and among over-65s by at least 33 per cent.

(All baselines 1990 except *1986 and **1989)

Risk factors reduction: Targets have been set for reductions in smoking, alcohol consumption, mean blood pressure in adults, obesity and consumption of saturated fats. A 10 per cent reduction in injecting drug users who share equipment has also been set.

---

or new health surveys and epidemiological overviews to improve baseline data on the health of the population will be undertaken. A Central Health Outcomes Unit will lead on developing and coordinating work on the assessment of health outcomes. Information systems which enable adequate monitoring and review will be developed including a Public Health Information Strategy.

Appraising the strategy

What is one to make of this initiative? Has the government seen the light on the road to Damascus and been converted to HFA? Obviously there is much to welcome about the White Paper. This is the most coherent attempt yet undertaken to give the NHS a positive health direction and to work out a detailed strategy for implementation. But the analysis is still fundamentally flawed by the ideological inability of the government to accept the centrality of poverty and social deprivation as causes of ill-health, and their political inability to take responsibility for policies which have widenened the numbers caught in its net.

The latest official figures show that the number of people living on incomes below half the national average (the nearest thing to an official poverty line) had increased from five million in 1979 when the Conservatives took office to 12 million in 1988/1989 (DSS 1992). The percentage of children living below this line was 25 compared with 10 per cent in 1979, indicating a total of 3.2 million children in poverty.

Income inequalities have widened. Over the same period the bottom 10 per cent saw their share of total income decline from 4.2 per cent to 3.2 per cent before housing costs are met, 4 per cent to 2.5 per cent after housing costs are accounted for. The growth in unemployment (again topping three million) is a major reason for the growth in poverty. The unemployed comprise 30 per cent of those in the bottom 10 per cent of income compared to 15 per cent in 1979.

Some of the other prerequisites of health have also worsened. Crime has soared, cars clog the roads and public transport needs massive investment. Homelessness has increased, yet councils are prevented from using the capital receipts from past council house sales to build social need housing. The ability of local authorities to fund voluntary groups and support community action (including Healthy City projects) is weakened by cuts in resources and powers.

There is little evidence that the government under John Major is any more willing than its predecessor to tackle these issues or reverse previous policies which have helped to create the problems in the first place. The tobacco advertising fiasco also induces scepticism about the true extent of the government's political commitment to health promotion and its ability to face down powerful lobbies among its friends and backers.

Turning to the arrangements for implementing the strategy, there are two fundamental concerns. First the ability of the government (or any government) to change the organisational culture of Whitehall away from departmentalism towards a corporate approach, and from short-termism to the long haul. The history of public policy is littered with the remains of good initiatives which never outlasted the Minister who promoted them.

Banning tobacco advertising

Smoking kills 110,000 people annually in the United Kingdom, and will account for 30 per cent of all deaths of those aged 35–69 throughout the developed world in the 1990s. To make up for these lost consumers, the United Kingdom tobacco industry has to recruit 300 new smokers every day. Inevitably these must be children and young people. There is sound evidence to show that cigarette advertising does get through to children, reinforces the smoking habit among those who already smoke, and encourages others to start. 'Brand stretching', associating cigarettes with other products like luxury goods or holidays, and tobacco sponsorship of sports and the arts, also works well with children (Hastings 1991).

In 1991 the European Community drafted proposals which would have:

1   Ended all tobacco advertising and promotion except in specialist tobacconist's shops;
2   Banned the promotion of tobacco through sponsorship of sport and the arts;
3   Stopped 'brand-stretching'.

There was widespread lobbying in favour of a 'yes' vote by health authorities, health pressure groups like Action on Smoking and Health, and professional bodies. Two thirds of the public already favoured such a ban in 1987 (Roberts and Smith 1987). The British government's support was vital in getting the proposal passed into legislation. It voted against, on the grounds that 'the Government remains to be convinced that a total ban will produce a significant reduction in smoking' (letter from Baroness Hooper, Under-Secretary of State for Health, 2.12.1991).

Yet the evidence from countries like Norway (which introduced a ban in 1975) and Australia (completed a total ban of media advertising by 1989) is quite clear. In Australia the ban on advertising is part of a comprehensive and effective package of anti-smoking measures. Wilkinson argues that the Australian government have acknowledged that 'governmental action does more to prolong life and prevent disease in this field than any other single factor' (Wilkinson 1992).

Norway's tobacco advertising ban has had a marked effect on the level of smoking among 13–15 year olds.

Britain has a poor record for long-term planning even for central economic policies in contrast to countries like Japan or Germany. If the new interdepartmental health committee can achieve genuine coordination of policy and institutionalise these arrangements to outlast the present government it will be a milestone in British politics.

Attempts in the 1970s to address strategic interdepartmental issues through the Central Policy Review Staff (the 'think-tank') and JASP (Joint Approach to Social Policy) were short-lived (Challis *et al.* 1988).

Hunter (1991b) suggests that one way the new committee could begin to institutionalise the health strategy in government is by requiring the publication of a 'health impact statement' from each department, assessing the health implications of their policies. (Similar 'health audits' have often been a feature of Healthy Cities projects at local level.) This would open up and inform public discussion and sensitise policy-makers on all the issues surrounding a particular health problem. Public support for health-promoting policies is growing stronger all the time as Healthy City activists know well, and Hunter argues that the committee must harness and build on this support to ensure continued political commitment. Politicians must see that health promotion wins votes.

Even more fundamentally, is the NHS the right agency to lead the health strategy in the first place? Some critics, including Hunter, argue that the NHS will never sufficiently free itself from medical definitions of health and medically driven priorities (although many doctors argue for just such a wider strategy, witness many recent articles in the *British Medical Journal*, for example, on such issues as poverty, the environment, tobacco advertising). Local authorities and the services they control or contract for have more impact on health than the health service. Giving the purchasing budget for health to a re-structured local government would make sense, both in terms of a wider health strategy, integrated health and social care and democratic accountability.

Clearly the argument is broadening to a wider look into the future, under this or future governments. What is the way ahead? Are there any clear pointers, or simply a muddle of contradictions? The final chapter will consider the evidence.

References

Altenstetter, C. (1989) 'Europe beyond 1992: implications for health and health policy', Paper prepared for European Community Studies Association Conference, May 24–25.

Ashton, J. (ed) (1992) *Healthy Cities*, Milton Keynes: Open University Press.

Ashton, J. and Seymour, H. (1988) *The New Public Health*, Milton Keynes: Open University Press.

Black, Sir Douglas (1980) *Inequalities in Health: Report of a research working group,* London : DHSS.

Blaxter, M. (1990) *Health and Lifestyles*, London: Tavistock/Routledge.

Challis, L. *et al.* (1988) *Joint Approaches to Social Policy*, Cambridge: Cambridge University Press.

Department of Health (1988) *Public Health in England: The Report of the Committee of Inquiry into the future development of the Public Health Function (The Acheson Report)*, Cmnd. 289, London: HMSO.

——(1991) *The Health of the Nation, A Consultative Document for Health in England*, Cmnd. 1523, London: HMSO.

——(1992) *The Health of the Nation*, Cmnd. 1986, London: HMSO

Department of Social Security (1992) *Households Below Average Income*, London: HMSO.

Dooris, M. (1987) 'Health for All by the Year 2000 in the United Kingdom', Unpublished dissertation for Diploma in Health Education, South Bank Polytechnic, London.

Draper, P. and Harrison, S. (1991) 'Prospects for healthy public policy' in P. Draper (ed) *Health through Public Policy*, London: Merlin Press.

Duhl, L.J. (1986) 'The healthy city: its function and its future', *Health Promotion*, 1: 55–60.

Graham, H. (1984) *Women, Health and the Family*, Brighton: Wheatsheaf

Hancock, T. (1988) 'Healthy Toronto 2000: a vision of a healthy city' in *Concepts and Visions – a Resource of the WHO Healthy Cities Project*, J. Ashton, Dept. of Community Health, University of Liverpool.

Hastings, G. (1991) 'The hard evidence against tobacco advertising', *Times Health Supplement*, Dec: 7–8.

Health Education Authority (1989) *Diet, Nutrition and Healthy Eating in Low Income Groups*, London: Health Education Authority.

Health Service Journal (1992) 'Smoking row looms as white paper rises from the ashes', 30 April: 5.

Hunter, D. (1991a) 'Beyond the NHS dilemma', *Health Service Journal*, 16 May 101 (5252): 26.

——(1991b) 'Breaking down barriers', *Health Service Journal*, 3 Oct, 101 (5272): 19.

Illsley, R. (1986) 'Occupational class, selection and the production of inequalities in health', *Quarter Journal of Social Affairs*, 2 (2) 151–165.

Illsley, R. and Le Grand, J. (1987) 'The measurement of inequality in health' in A. Williams (ed) *Economics and Health*, London: Macmillan.

Jones, I.A. (1992) 'An investigation into the factors affecting the diet of low income groups', Unpublished Dissertation for B.Sc. Hons. in Applied Consumer Science, University of Northumbria.

Kickbusch, I. (1989) 'Approaches to an ecological base for public health', *Health Promotion* 4: 4.

Klein, R. (1988) 'Acceptable inequalities' in D. Green (ed) *Acceptable Inequalities? Essays on the Pursuit of Equality in Healthcare*, London: Institute of Economic Affairs.

Lalonde, M. (1974) A new perspective on the health of Canadians, Ottawa: Government of Canada.

Lang, T. and Cole-Hamilton, I. (1986) *Tightening Belts – A Report on the Impact of Poverty on Food*, 2nd edn, London: London Food Commission.

MacDonald, A. and Hanes, F.A. (1988) 'Can I afford the diet?', *Journal of Human Nutrition and Dietetics*: 389–96.

Marmot, M.G. and McDowall, M.E. (1986) 'Mortality decline and widening social inequalities', *Lancet*, 2: 274–6.

National Advisory Council for Nutrition Education (1983) *A Discussion Paper for Proposals for Nutrition Guidelines for Health Education in Britain*, London: Health Education Council

Newby, H. (1983) 'Living from hand to mouth: the farmworker, food and agribusiness' in A. Murcott (ed) *The Sociology of Food and Eating*, Aldershot: Gower.

Newcastle District Health Authority (1988) *Coronary heart disease prevention policy Health Promotion and Illness Prevention Policy Group*, 3 November, Newcastle upon Tyne.

——(1990) *Health and ill-health in Newcastle upon Tyne: First report of the Director of Public Health*, Newcastle upon Tyne.

Robbins, C. (1991) 'Our manufactured diet' in P. Draper (ed) *Health through Public Policy*, London: Merlin Press.

Roberts, J. and Smith, C. (1987) 'Public health promoted', *Health Service Journal*, 22 Sept: 1230–1.

Tannahill, A. (1987) 'Regional health promotion planning and monitoring', *Health Education Journal*, 46 (3): 125–7.

Townsend, P. Phillimore, P. and Beattie, A. (1987) *Health and Deprivation: Inequality and the North*, London: Croom Helm.

Townsend, P. (1990a) 'Widening inequalities of health in Britain: A rejoinder to Rudolf Klein', *International Journal of Health Services*, 20 (3): 363–72.

——(1990b) 'Individual or social responsibility for premature death? The current controversies in the British debate about health', *International Journal of Health Services*, 20 (3): 373–92 .

Thunhurst, C. (1991) 'Information and Public Health', in P. Draper (ed) *Health through Public Policy*, London: Merlin Press.

Tsouros, A. (ed) (1991) *WHO Healthy Cities Project: A Project Becomes a Movement*, Copenhagen: WHO Regional Office for Europe.

Whichelow, M.J. (1987) *The Health and Lifestyle Survey*, London: Health Promotion Research Trust.

Whitehead, M. (1987) *The Health Divide*, London: Health Education Council.

Wilkinson, R.G. (1986) 'Occupational class, selection and inequalities in health: a reply to Raymond Illsley', *Quarterly Journal of Social Affairs*, 2 (4): 415–22.

——(1989) 'Class mortality differentials, income distribution and trends in poverty 1921–1981' *Journal of Social Policy* l8 (3): 307–37.

Wilkinson, T. (1992) 'Smoke signals', *Health Service Journal*, 30 April: 28–9.

Wilson, G. (1989) 'Family food systems, preventive health and dietary change: a policy to increase the health divide', *Journal of Social Policy* 18 (2): 167–85.

——(1987) *Money in the Family: Financial Organisation and Women's Responsibility*, Aldershot: Avebury.

World Health Organisation (1946) *Constitution*, Geneva: WHO.

——(1978) *Alma Ata: Primary Health Care*, Geneva: WHO.

——(1981) *Global Strategy for Health for All by the Year 2000* ('Health for All' Series No. 3). Geneva: WHO.

——(1985) *Targets for Health for All*, Copenhagen: WHO Regional Office for Europe.

——(1986) *Ottawa Charter for Health Promotion*, Copenhagen: WHO.

——(1988) *The Work of WHO in the European Region 1987, Annual Report of the Regional Director*, Copenhagen: WHO Regional Office for Europe.

CHAPTER 9

Future directions

There is no clear path to the goal of Health for All. Instead we must 'muddle through to Utopia' in Trevor Hancock's words (Hancock 1991). In practice this needs firmness of purpose combined with flexible tactics, recognising that there will be retreats and sidesteps on the way. In any case the scale of social change and uncertainty has made planning in the old sense of linear programmed progress along a predetermined route obsolete. It must give way to continual social learning and experiment, and planning as an emergent flexible process. Creativity and lateral thinking, the ability to reframe old problems and synthesise apparent contradictions, is as important as reason and logic.

But goal-directed 'muddling through' still requires a strategic analysis of major trends which shape the context of policy and present different opportunities and threats, some of which have been explored in previous chapters.

The changing environment of health care

The NHS in the 1990s faces a policy context which has changed dramatically in some respects in recent years, but is only too depressingly familiar in others.

The restructuring of welfare

Thirteen years of Conservative rule have transformed the provision and organisation of welfare in Britain according to a broad set of principles.

1   Greater fragmentation of service delivery, regulatory and strategic responsibilities.
2   Commitment to competition.
3   Separating the responsibility for a service from direct provision (the purchaser-provider split in health and social welfare, local management of schools).
4   Greater scope for commercial, voluntary and informal provision – the 'mixed economy of welfare'.
5   Increased emphasis on the 'safety net' role of state welfare with

individuals and families encouraged to 'top up' or replace state provision through private pensions, private education, health insurance, student loans.

6 A commitment to greater consumer choice and explicit consumer rights (the Citizen's Charter and its offshoots).

7 An attack on the power of producer interest groups. Public sector unions and professional groups have had their influence checked. This has been achieved both directly, by more 'flexible' employment conditions, performance-related pay, and the erosion of national pay bargaining machinery, and indirectly through the introduction of market forces.

8 A 'managerialist' approach to the organisation and running of welfare agencies which borrows much from the commercial sector.

9 A weakening of traditional intermediate centres of power (local representative democracy, trade unions) and the attempt to empower individuals directly as consumers, patients, parents, tenants.

10 New forms of accountability to the centre, for example through explicit performance and spending targets, new or strengthened monitoring mechanisms (accountability reviews in the NHS, extended role of the Audit Commission, development of performance indicators).

(adapted from Stewart and Stoker 1989: 2–5)

As Cochrane (1992) points out, the process of restructuring is still not fully worked out and hence it is difficult to predict the results of a complex and diverse set of processes, but the election of the Conservatives in 1992 makes it probable that these developments will strengthen further over the next four years.

At a local level, the 'local state' is becoming a more crowded and contested field. Business has been given a much more important role, but in addition a wealth of nonelected statutory and voluntary agencies have entered the field as major or minor players. Many of them are in the health field (for example, NHS trusts, FHSAs, housing associations as providers of residential care). The traditional local power centre, the local authority, has been weakened and there is considerable debate about its future role. Nevertheless the broad trend towards welfare pluralism is clear cut: government as the main service provider is giving way to government by contract and regulation.

Although the specific form restructuring has taken reflects the ideological principles of the New Right, larger trends in society are also involved, and parallel organisational changes are already apparent in manufacturing and service industry (what loosely might be called post-Fordist developments).

A changing intellectual paradigm

The heyday of the therapeutic era and the medical model of health may well be drawing to a close. Socio-ecological concepts of health and illness have exerted a powerful intellectual challenge, underpinning a renewed and expanded public health movement. Paradoxically the very advance of medical technologies and techniques seem to strengthen the arguments for a public health approach to health gain. Governments throughout the Western world are aware that they face a widening gap between what is possible and what is affordable in healthcare. This is leading to a much greater stress on evaluating the benefits and costs of health care interventions, both new and existing technologies, and renewed interest in preventive strategies and health promotion.

Radical critics of health promotion argue that to date the focus on prevention has largely taken an individualistic victim-blaming stance, with its emphasis on life-styles and choice to the neglect of social, economic and environmental determinants of health. Medical concepts of health and disease have not been overturned, they claim, simply given a new twist. While there is considerable truth in this view the weight of evidence supporting a socio-ecological model of health is now becoming so overwhelming that governments of different ideological persuasions, albeit at different speeds and with different degrees of reluctance, are beginning to accept its validity and face up to the policy implications.

Changing the focus of health care delivery

The thousand-bedded district general hospital will become an anachronism in the twenty-first century. Primary and community health services will almost certainly grow in importance at the expense of hospital services, partly in response to consumerist and resource pressures: much of what is presently done in hospitals could more conveniently and cheaply be done in general practice or primary health centres. But the trend is also driven by the ageing of the population and associated changes in the pattern of health needs as well as the established professional consensus on best practice for the long-term care of the elderly, and those with chronic mental and physical disabilities.

The high-tech hospital of the future will probably have no more than four hundred beds, one quarter of them in intensive care (Loughton 1992). Lengths of stay will continue to fall, and technological advance will allow much more day surgery. Small community hospitals, 'hospitals at home', or patient hotels will take over as sites for recuperation and rehabilitation. Once again decentralisation and diversity are the underlying principles but, as bureaucracies give way to networks, considerable investment in information technology is still required to ensure efficient administration, personalised service and continuity of patient care.

Continuing resource constraints

Resource constraints of both people and money will continue to figure prominently in the next few years. Although the severity of skill shortages experienced by the NHS has temporarily been masked by the depth of the recession and unemployment, nevertheless they will re-emerge given the labour market and social expenditure implications of the changing age structure of the population. In response, human resource management in the NHS will assume greater importance. The pressure for more flexible modes of working will lead to greater experimentation with skill mixes. Old demarcation barriers between professions and subprofessions may dissolve, while new ones are created. Multiskilling and deskilling may be happening at the same time for different categories of staff. (An example is the creation of a new elite of paramedically trained ambulance workers and the demotion of others to the status of general drivers, competing for contracts with private transport firms.) More services will be subject to market testing and put out to contract.

In terms of expenditure, the 'greying' of the population makes heavy demands on health and social care and on pensions. High unemployment worsens the actual 'dependency ratio' (the ratio between the working and nonworking population) and adds further to the social welfare budget. The immediate economic outlook is depressing with the weakest and most fragile of recoveries forecast for 1993–94. Although the Chancellor's Autumn Statement did not produce the swingeing cuts in the welfare budget which had been forecast for 1993–94, the settlement for the NHS is only 0.8 per cent above the inflation forecast. The NHS seems set for a rerun of the financial stringency of the mid-1980s in spite of political commitments to 'quality' public services.

NHS budgets will also feel the 'knock-on' effects of cuts in local authority services. Ironically as the philosophy of a 'wider health strategy' wins greater acceptance, local authorities are in the business of closing community swimming pools, leisure centres, residential homes and day centres. Although collaboration is more necessary than ever, health authorities may find collaboration with local authorities more difficult as they become embroiled in their own internal difficulties of managing cuts, implementing the new Council Tax, and getting to grips with community care.

The political and ideological context

Shortly after the 1992 election, some political commentators claimed that 'Majorism' signalled a move back to one-nation Toryism and more consensual interventionist policies. Both the social consequences of Thatcherism and the economic failures of excessive reliance on free market economics had forced the Conservatives to retreat back onto centre ground. However, the evidence is mixed. The party is deeply divided and the government's policies increasingly lack coherence or a clear set of principles as the government lurches from one crisis to another. Many of its policies could still be termed 'Thatcherite', and reflect a continuing dogmatic commitment to privatisation and free market economics in areas where the case for such policies is extremely weak, for example, British Rail, The Post Office or Prison Service.

At the same time the Labour Party has had to come to terms with the results of 13 years of Conservative rule and the prospect of four more, including the enormous changes introduced into the organisation and provision of welfare. The old instinctive Fabian hostility to markets is giving way to more measured and sophisticated consideration about what types of market relations are appropriate in what kind of circumstances, and with what degree of regulation.

The collapse of Communism as a major contending economic philosophy may aid this debate, since it is clear that the old dichotomy between Communism and capitalism was a myth. There are many variants of capitalism operating in conjunction with different types of political system from Scandinavian social democracy to North Korean autocracy. Some of the most successful capitalist economies, like Germany and Japan, have demonstrated that there is no necessary antithesis between markets and planning and that the state has a key role in setting the political and normative framework within which the efficiency-promoting virtues of markets are played out.

On the health service the differences between the parties are not as wide in substance as they appear to be in rhetoric. There is still a wide measure of agreement that the goals of the NHS are to promote the health of the population and respond to need. Both of these goals are quite consistent with the direction of current policy, if need is interpreted as 'the capacity to benefit from health care' (Maynard 1991: 17).

Differences on the means to achieve these goals are also not as wide as they appear. For example, many of the Labour Party's criticisms of the *Health of the Nation* Green Paper had been taken on board by the Conservatives in the White Paper, though the Labour Party would have given greater prominence to the issue of health inequalities and be more ready to take legislative action on issues like tobacco advertising, for example. There are few differences on the thrust of community care policy, especially since the Conservatives have 'ring-fenced' the community care budget to local authorities, although Labour would probably change the financial rules which favour providers in the private sector. The Labour Party promised before the election to begin to remedy underfunding of the health service as resources allowed, but they would have been hampered by the size of the public spending borrowing requirement they inherited and the economic straitjacket of the slump.

The most important pre-election difference was Labour's intention to abolish managed competition. Instead they proposed that community health authorities, forged from existing DHAs and FHSAs, would remain responsible for meeting the health needs of their resident populations but GP fundholding and NHS trusts would go. Services would be brought back under health authority control, albeit at arms length, and contracts replaced by performance agreements with incentive payments for those meeting the health authority's targets. It was unclear, however, how these would work in practice. The referral rights of GPs were respected and they would be given a role in vetting health authority contracts in compensation for the loss of fundholding freedoms. In short, even though the Labour Party disliked the internal market, it was still trying to retain the benefits of the purchaser–provider split and the increased power of GPs by other means.

NHS reforms – the current state of play

The Conservative victory in 1992 ensured that the main features of the NHS reforms would stay in place. By April 1994 all but a small rump of services will have trust status. One in four patients will be registered with a GP practice which holds its own hospital budget by April 1993, and fundholders can now purchase a range of community services as well. Although no legislative plans to integrate FHSAs and DHAs have been announced, there is much informal merger movement either instigated by RHAs or through 'bottom-up' decisions by individual groups of authorities. This may involve straight DHA merger as well as DHA/FHSA liaisons. Apart from formal mergers there are a large number of consortia arrangements in place, some of them covering a range of DHAs, FHSA and local authority purchasers. GP fundholders have also combined in consortia arrangements to maximise their bargaining leverage with providers and reduce administration costs, and consortia of up to 70 GPs have emerged.

There may be advantages in mergers and consortia through the more economic use of scarce and expensive skills (such as public health medicine and information specialists), greater scope for both competition and complementarity of services, greater bargaining leverage with providers and easier collaboration across agency boundaries. However often the advantages and disadvantages of mergers have not been thought through and restructuring usually causes as many problems as it solves (remoteness from local communities, for example). It takes a considerable toll of people and relationships even when voluntarily undertaken, and the disruption may outweigh any potential benefit for a long time. Nor is it a substitute for the hard patient work required to establish trust and confidence between different agencies and between agencies and the people they serve, which is necessary whatever administrative pattern is chosen.

Three clear roles have emerged in the new managed market: regulator, provider and purchaser. How have these developed, and what is the relationship between them?

RHAs have developed as the regulators of 'managed competition' with important roles in setting the overall framework of health goals and quality standards for providers and purchasers, managing the pace of change and arbitrating in disputes. However the role requires a skilful balance between central control and allowing local autonomy – a balance which few RHAs have managed successfully. In January 1993, Mrs Bottomley reaffirmed that streamlined RHAs would continue to play the watchdog role for the immediate future, but with a lighter touch.

The provider role is relatively clear-cut and seems to have developed fastest, particularly where units are already trusts. Controversy still exists about trusts. Some argue (as the Labour Party did before the election) that the benefits of the purchaser–provider split can be achieved by decentralisation rather than separation, and criticise trusts for behaving like commercial organisations rather than publicly funded bodies. Increased autonomy has been matched by reduced accountability.

Furthermore, as budgetary pressures return to their usual severity after a two-year pre-election bonus there will be intense pressures for trusts to maximise their incomes by shedding unprofitable services or expanding their private provision, with the consequent dangers of a two-tier service. A second Rubber Windmill role-play exercise in 1992 demonstrated a third problem. The existence of a large number of independent or semi-independent organisations makes the restructuring of services under the name of health gain (from hospital to primary care, for instance) more difficult to handle (East Anglian RHA/OPM 1992) since each hospital fights to protect its own interests.

These dangers have to be weighed against evidence which suggests that health authorities find it difficult to develop a strong purchasing role when they continue to have managerial responsibility for their units. Conceptually the role is confused and in practice both sides face tensions over issues of power and control in what remains a hierarchical relationship. Purchasers are continually trying to wear two hats in contract negotiations, and become embroiled once again in managing services and patients rather than concentrating on health and people. Unless there is an unusually strong degree of devolution already, complete separation seems to be necessary before the work of re-establishing a new kind of relationship based on different assumptions and roles can begin. Now, even the Labour Party has accepted that trusts are here to stay, but would like to strengthen their accountability to the local community.

One of the most significant developments reported by all the provider units in the 'Monitoring Managed Competition' case study districts was a 'sea change' in medical attitudes, which was attributed to the fact that if they did not provide a service 'the patients vote with their feet and go elsewhere' (Ranade 1993). In general this was leading to more corporate working with managers as well as the breakdown of professional barriers. The rate and pace of change differed between districts and consultants and the impetus for change sometimes came from GP fundholders rather than district purchasers. Nevertheless respondents in all the districts saw this as a highly significant longterm development which had given greater impetus to clinicians in management. Systems of clinical management were being installed where they had not existed before to underpin contracting, resource management and medical audit, and had become part of the accepted way of doing things in those hospitals which had a head start. One trust Chief Executive argued that it was no longer his job to manage the hospital: 'What I do is oversee it, I keep my finger on it but very arm's length. My job now is to manage the external environment, it is not to manage the internal one.' One of his clinical directors was of the same mind: 'to be in charge of my destiny . . . that's the concrete benefit. I always knew the right people to run a hospital were the doctors and nurses and I am absolutely convinced of it now'.

It is interesting to speculate where these developments could lead. It is perfectly possible that the present dual system of general and medical management could become redundant in 10 years time, if sufficient doctors decided to specialise in management and take on the relevant training. Such a trend would parallel developments which have already occurred in the United States (see, for instance, McKinlay and Stoekle 1988).

Having more control over their own affairs seems to have liberated many providers and released a lot of creative energy. Often they take the lead in suggesting new services or patterns of care. Strongly managed trusts are looking to expand in other directions (developing outreach hospital services, for example) or run services in other districts, perhaps through a management franchise. How this is viewed depends on one's point of view: market takeovers by powerful competitors or more effective use of managerial leadership? The criteria for evaluation should be the benefits and costs to patients and local communities and it may take some time for these to be known.

The purchasing function, by contrast, has developed more slowly and weakly across the board. Although this is the heart of the health service reforms there was no clear understanding of this at first at government level and therefore no clear leadership. The association of purchasing with an enlarged and strategic public health role for health authorities is only gradually taking shape through a learning-by-doing approach on the ground. It is hardly surprising that the development has been slow. In the first year of the reforms authorities were preoccupied with the mechanics of contracting and trying to align information systems to support the new way of doing business. Inexperience meant too much effort went into the specifics of the contract and too little into thinking through the basis of the relationship with suppliers, particularly their own units. In the words of one rather amused UGM who had a background of contract negotiation in the engineering industry: 'Contracts are a worthless bit of paper . . . it's the intent behind the contract that matters'.

In the second year of contracting, many DHAs started to express their dissatisfaction or frustrations (often long-standing) with existing providers, and were determined to make changes with little regard for their effects on providers. Unilateral action could impose damaging cuts in workload or activity, which could raise unit costs, and make certain services uneconomic. Attitudes towards service change (a more rapid build-up of community services for example) became more entrenched as hospitals fought for survival, and regions were called in to arbitrate as relationships between purchasers and providers took a nose dive. A nervous NHSME made matters worse by requiring DHAs to declare their purchasing intentions for 1992–93 when the 1991–92 contracts had run for barely six months.

The effects were most clearly seen in London, as referrals to hospitals from out-of-London districts dropped, triggering the Tomlinson Inquiry into the future of London's health services and the subsequent recommendation that some of the most prestigious teaching hospitals should close or merge (Tomlinson 1992). Similar problems developed on a smaller scale in some other cities like Newcastle and Birmingham. Market pressures had pushed long-standing problems back up the agenda and made them impossible to ignore, but illustrated the fact that restructuring services and closing hospitals will always require political courage and a planned and coordinated approach over a number of years to do well.

Changing views about the purchasing role are reflected in changed terminology. 'Purchasing' became 'commissioning' – the difference is neatly described by one director of purchasing as: 'I liken purchasing to going into a supermarket and buying what is on the shelves, and commissioning to deciding what ought to go on the shelves in the first place'. Parston however argues that even the term 'commissioning' does not fully reflect the role of the purchaser, which he describes as fundamentally a public health role, working to assure the health of the population (Parston 1991). To do this, health assurers have to work closely with providers, the public and politicians in providing information, finding incentives to change attitudes and ways of working, developing new services, cutting back old ones. Efficiency pressures will continue to be as important as the pressures for more effective and responsive services and health assurers have to lead the local dialogue on what are acceptable trade offs in values, Oregon-style.

One promising development to aid this work is the establishment of a Research and Development strategy by the Department of Health, headed by a Director at the level of NHSME, and the commitment to spend 1½ per cent of the NHS budget on research. A key element of this strategy will be the evaluation of health services and treatments, giving a substantial nationally-led boost to the information available to guide both purchasers and providers.

This view of purchasing is very different from the original concept in WFP, shopping in the market place for the best buy. Competition does not disappear, however, it adds tension at the margins to keep everyone on their toes and provide comparative information for use in negotiations. The threat of going elsewhere is a weapon of last resort.

But if purchasers are to 'assure' the health of their local populations, this requires at the very least agreement on priorities between DHA, FHSA and GPs and coordinated if not joint health plans. Is this possible when purchasing is divided between DHAs and GP fundholders?

The pros and cons of GP fundholding

Enthoven's original proposals did not envisage GP fundholding. Instead DHAs would have contracted for primary care with GPs as providers, making FHSAs redundant. Now there are two models of purchasing: one based on individual demands and 'consumer choice' and the other based on the needs of populations and public health. Both have their advocates. Glennerster's research with 10 first wave practices in three regions in the South East of England (Glennerster *et al.* 1992), supplemented later by a sample of second and third wave practices, is broadly supportive of GP fundholding because:

1 GPs are closer to their patients and more responsive to their needs than DHAs;
2 They have greater independence than DHAs and have made the market work quickly and effectively, making gains for their patients which are highly appreciated;
3 GP fundholders have a stronger incentive than their non-fundholding colleagues to pursue more efficient methods of treatment. In Glennerster's research, GPs negotiated agreements with consultants on issues like the number of return outpatient appointments, discharge procedures or alternative drug regimes for particular conditions.

It could be argued that making GPs the primary purchaser also accords with the emphasis on primary care in HFA and in government policy. This has intensified with the recent decision to enlarge the range of services that GPs can purchase. From April 1993 these have included community services like district nursing, health visiting, community and outpatient mental health services, services for people with learning disabilities, chiropody and dietetics. But there are many actual and potential problems associated with GP purchasing.

1 As the number of fundholders increases, DHAs lose a correspondingly greater share of their budget. This makes it difficult to balance demands for emergency versus elective care.
2 Widening the number of semi-independent 'stakeholders' makes planning more difficult and undermines the DHA's ability to meet *Health of the Nation* and Patient Charter targets and the local authority's responsibility for community care services.
3 The gains made by first wave fundholders may not be replicable by all. In particular inner-city poorer practices may be further disadvantaged.
4 Fragmenting contracting by individual practices is wasteful of time and money. There seems little point in developing fundholding consortia to overcome this problem when health authorities exist to do the job already and have the necessary administrative support.
5 Inequities are likely, given the problems of 'cream skimming' and the imprecision of allocating budgets down to practice populations.

Which way forward?

There is now a growing degree of consensus internationally on what the desirable macro goals of health policy should be and the systemic features which best promote them. A recent OECD survey of health reforms in seven countries including the United Kingdom (Hurst and Poullier 1993) concludes that the goals are:

1 Adequacy and equity of access and a fair funding system;
2 Macro-economic efficiency – ensuring health care consumes an appropriate share of GDP;
3 Micro efficiency – maximising a chosen mix of improvements in health and in consumer satisfaction for a given share of GDP spent on health;
4 Freedom of choice for consumers;
5 A sufficient degree of autonomy for professional providers.

The NHS traditionally scored well on the first two, less well on three and four and reasonably well on the fifth. In addition there are other desirable policy goals suggested by the discussion in previous chapters:

1 A public health approach to health improvement;
2 Greater accountability to the public and a more democratic ethos;
3 Reducing health inequalities;
4 A primary care-led service.

How can this mix of objectives be best attained? There is now considerable evidence that financing the bulk of health care from public funds is the best way to safeguard equity and access, with voluntary insurance or private payments restricted to a supplementary role (Ham *et al.* 1990; Hurst and Poullier 1993). Cost containment is most easily achieved through globally capped budgets on providers, another strength of the British system. However there seems to be a strong case for a modest increase in the percentage of GDP Britain spends on health care. If extra monies were carefully targeted to improve user satisfaction it would lessen tendencies to exit to the private sector (Ham *et al*. 1990) and GP fundholders have shown that the improvements most appreciated by the public do not necessarily cost a great deal.

The 'underfunding' issue has been a muted subtheme in this book because adopting a social model of health requires resources to be invested elsewhere to achieve bigger health gains. No-one could dispute, for example, that putting the unemployed back to work would do more to improve health than spending an extra couple of billion pounds on the health service. But the cash pressures which the NHS is once again experiencing could intensify incentives for private sector growth and at the same time lead to infighting between providers – the Rubber Windmill exercise still stands as an ominous warning. Extra finance will also be necessary to smooth the transition from a hospital-based to a primary and community-based health care system and to invest in the information systems which are required.

Ironically, if government commitment to quality public services had been present in the 1980s these changes would have been easier to achieve since fiscal revenues were buoyant. Now that they are falling and GDP shrinking it may mean testing the public's willingness to bear a greater tax burden to support the NHS, perhaps through a hypothecated Health Tax.

The achievement of other objectives is also bound up with the development of managed competition and the NHS reforms. These are now at a critical stage, and could develop in several directions either by design or default. The discussion concentrates on two aspects: the development of the commissioning role and improving choice and accountability.

Strengthening commissioning

The commissioning role is the key to the NHS reforms, which has to drive the rest. If this remains underdeveloped and weakened by heavy handed top-down control on one hand and the fragmenting effect of GP fundholding on the other, the promise of the new public health will be lost. This suggests that the best solution is a combined DHA/FHSA, purchasing primary and secondary care, relating to GPs mainly as providers but in ways which try to retain the undoubted benefits that fundholders have introduced.

Commissioning needs a two-tier approach. A commitment to participation and responsiveness requires detailed consultation and knowledge of local needs and wishes: a commitment to equity means that final decisions on priorities must be taken on an authority-wide basis, balancing the needs and claims of different local areas and client groups. Several authorities have experimented with forms of locality purchasing to reconcile these competing demands. These involve decentralising a number of functions to 'localities' which may be based on small towns or communities, GP practices or groups of electoral wards. The objectives and management arrangements vary, although there is a broad agreement that the tasks to be carried out at locality level include needs assessment, relating to GPs and local people, liaising with other agencies and working with providers.

In Stockport, for example, an important objective for the DHA and FHSA is to implement a primary care-led approach to secondary care purchasing. GPs give advice and information about needs to the local 'health strategy manager' who covers a population of about 50,000 and give their views on the placing of contracts. In turn the local manager acts as a trouble shooter for GPs, taking up their concerns with providers and helping to iron out problems. But although GPs are an important source of information, they are but one group among many and the health strategy manager works with a variety, helping to give meaning to the concept of 'local voices' (Ham 1992).

In North Derbyshire and Bath localities are based on existing GP practices and an alternative approach based on 'practice sensitive purchasing' is being piloted. Both authorities are exploring the feasibility of mirroring GP fundholding by devolving notional budgets to practices so that they can influence purchasing decisions, while at the same time involving GPs in a dialogue on priorities and equitable principles of allocating resources.

Both of these approaches are an alternative to fundholding which can be acceptable to GPs without jeopardising a wider strategy, but a locality approach can also mitigate the disadvantages of larger purchasing authorities. The different experiments taking place need careful evaluation and dissemination.

Improving accountability and choice

Recent arguments about improving the accountability of public services tend to polarise into two positions. The present government's view is that this is best achieved by individual choice in the 'mixed economy of welfare', coupled with enhanced consumer rights and entitlements as laid down in the various Citizen's Charters. An alternative view, argued by many across a broad centre-left spectrum, is to improve collective choice in the polity by strengthening the democratic process, either by giving citizens more opportunities to participate directly in the policy-making process or through strengthening representative channels. The two views are not necessarily antithetical. Improving choice in the 'managed market' and creating stronger democratic mechanisms can be complementary strategies.

Improving consumer choice

Saltmann and Von Otter (1992) argue that direct consumer choice of hospital and consultant would start to change the balance of forces and make patients rather than managers the agent of change in the managed market. Money really would follow the patient rather than patients following the contract. This would also enhance the legitimacy of managerial decisions (to reduce the funding for a particular hospital, for example) and the accountability of providers. In this version of the 'planned market', however, competition is restricted to public providers, and funding mechanisms would have to change.

Saltmann and Von Otter argue there would be other advantages from greater consumer choice:

1 Competition would be quality-led rather than finance driven and users would become the monitors of quality in those areas they are competent to judge. Consumer choice takes place within the present parameters of cash-limited budgets however, and should not lead to increased expenditure, simply a redistribution among providers.
2 If users have more choice within the public sector, they will have less incentive to demonstrate dissatisfaction by exiting to the private sector.
3 Widening consumer choice is a popular move and particularly advantages users who do not possess the time, desire or skills to participate in other ways.

Although extending consumer choice to secondary care is desirable Saltmann and Von Otter may be exaggerating the benefits it can bring. They admit that the exigencies of geography and the location of specialities already impose natural limits in most cases and inevitably most consumers will still rely on their GP's advice. Also these kind of choices are largely confined to elective surgical procedures, and do not encompass wider issues about the structure of services or funding priorities. These require other methods of gauging consumer opinion and ensuring accountable decision-making.

Strengthening the democratic process

Local democratic accountability in the NHS has always been weak. The members of health authorities were either appointed by the RHA for their individual experience and expertise, or were nominees of local councils, medical and nursing consultative bodies, trade unions and universities. In practice their role was confused – part managerial part representative – and a number of studies found that their influence on policy was slight in comparison with full-time officers. Since

September 1990 these have been replaced by smaller, tightly knit boards of mixed executive and nonexecutive directors which may be more effective managerially but are even less accountable to local people. For example, there has been a decline in the number of meetings held in public. Trust boards, modelled on similar lines, operate with even greater secrecy and fewer than one in fifteen trusts allows a CHC representative to board meetings (Ashburner and Cairncross 1992).

This decline in accountability is part of a larger problem. Stewart points out that the growing fragmentation of public administration at local level confuses the public, who do not know where responsibility lies and whom to call to account when things go wrong. Many believe, for example, that local authorities are responsible for hospitals and hardly anyone knows the names or responsibilities of health authority members (Stewart 1993).

The easiest way to strengthen the democratic legitimacy of health authorities is to transfer the commissioning role to local authorities. In the longer term this is an attractive option, but it seems neither feasible nor desirable for a number of years, even if there was any chance of the present government considering the possibility. Local government is itself being restructured in a piecemeal way by the Local Government Commission, a process which may take at least three years.

There are also doubts revolving round the culture of local government and the present deficiencies of representative democracy. Most councils have hardly begun to make the profound cultural shift involved in fitting services to people, rather than the reverse, managing the purchaser–provider split and the mixed economy of welfare. They are ill-equipped to take on major new responsibilities for health commissioning for some time. Even if they did there is little evidence that this by itself would lead to a more democratic policy process. Similar hopes guided reformers in Norway, when primary health care responsibilities were fully devolved to municipalities in 1984, but policy-making there is still confined to a narrow range of specialist officers and professionals (Elstad 1990). Changing the culture of local and health authorities is the pre-requisite of further organisational change, and far more energy should be devoted to bringing this about.

It is precisely the deficiencies of representative democracy that lead to recurrent interest in stimulating new forms of participatory or direct democracy. But many social scientists rightly regard the word 'participation' with great suspicion. Political rhetoric and sloppy usage have devalued the concept, and the recent history of practical experiments in participation is very mixed. (Good reviews of these can be found in Cochrane 1986; see also Croft and Beresford 1992.) Nevertheless such experiments provide valuable lessons for the present. The first lesson is that participation can be manipulated to serve a variety of self-serving ends. To be genuine there must be real commitment by powerholders to create the means for the more active involvement of ordinary citizens in the policy process.

The second lesson is to be clear about the aims and objectives of participation. In the new NHS these might be:

1 To create a user-led service by finding ways of changing the nature of the relationship between users and providers to one of partnership;
2 To give citizens a more effective say in the development and management of services;
3 To help people develop the skills and knowledge necessary to take more control of their own health;
4 To develop policies and services which support people's civil rights, and safeguard equality of access.

Another important lesson is to begin modestly and not to foster unrealistic expectations which cannot be met. Creating a climate of trust, especially among those who have learnt to expect little from officialdom, requires the results of participation to be demonstrable (see Winkler 1991 for some imaginative suggestions).

Different forms of 'bottom-up' participation such as the consumer councils and local forums mentioned in Chapter 7, or experiments in locality commissioning, can be supplemented by other ways of fostering an open and accountable service. At the national level, the deliberations of the Policy Board need to be more transparent. As Lewis and Longley (1993) point out present secrecy means that: 'It is difficult to estimate to what extent the Policy Board actually influences policy as opposed to legitimising what the Secretary of State already has in mind' (p. 26).

At the local level, nonexecutive directors and chairs of authorities and trusts should be chosen according to stringent equal opportunity procedures, giving everyone a fair chance instead of relying on old boys' networks. Information pamphlets on what the posts involve should be freely available in public places and expressions of interest requested in the press. A pool of potential candidates could be given preliminary training to ensure people fully understood what membership involves. All applicants should be interviewed and appointments made against specified criteria. However at least one of the members should be a senior councillor, to ease the collaborative aspects of financing and planning community care at board level, even though in practice there is a good deal of overlapping membership of working parties and committees at other levels.

Trust boards could institutionalise the links they have with the local community by establishing a number of policy committees along Canadian lines to consider specific areas such as quality assurance, service development or equal opportunities, which would include as members informed people from the community (Rathwell 1992).

The information that DHAs and trusts are required to make public should be rethought, within the context of a Freedom of Information bill. Community Health Councils should be given more status and resources to carry out their important role as the patient's watchdog, and complaints meticulously analysed and indeed treasured for the general lessons they convey. There should be a clearer specification of accountability relationships between executive and nonexecutive members, and different levels of authority. For example, if Chief Executives of DHAs retain the confidence of their board, in what circumstances do Regional General Managers have the right to remove them?

Strengthening accountability and creating a culture which supports an open and democratic ethos have been given particular attention here because the reality gives such cause for concern.

In 1992 there were major scandals in two RHAs, at least one involving fraud, leading to the loss of hundreds of thousands of pounds in IT contracts. Trust managers have suspended or dismissed staff who publicly complained about poor quality of care on behalf of their patients, forcing the Secretary of State to publish a 'whistle blower's charter' to protect future complainants. RHAs have merged districts and moved managers like pawns on a chess board, getting rid of those who were of an inconveniently independent mind. A similar fate has befallen some chairs and nonexecutive members whose only crime was a failure always to agree with the regional Chair. Intolerance of opposition and dissent has reached disturbing proportions. Instead of upholding and cherishing values which support public service, professional commitment and managerial honesty, in some regions and districts they were trampled underfoot creating demoralisation, cynicism and distress.

Conclusions – creating the learning culture

The NHS reforms contained the seeds of a more dynamic, responsive and efficient health service, and in the concept of the 'health assurer' the means by which public health can be reinvigorated. But that potential will be lost unless there is a commitment to social learning at every level of the organisation. In his brilliant book, *Images of Organisation*, Gareth Morgan (1986) uses the metaphor of the organisation as a brain, open to stimuli from the environment through all its senses but able to focus its attention at will and capable of reflecting and learning from experience. To become a genuine learning organisation, however, the NHS must be open to dissent and critical enquiry. The requirements both of healthy democracy and good management demand it. Learning cannot flourish in a climate of fear or cynicism, when good news is politically manufactured or criticism branded as disloyalty.

If the NHS was truly a learning organisation the development of managed competition would be guided by the experience of other countries as well as the diversity of experiment taking place here. There are particularly useful lessons on how the market can be designed to ensure that the private sector remains complementary to the NHS, and does not undermine equity and access. In their review of six countries, Ham *et al.* (1990) conclude that if the state provides the bulk of the finance and guarantees access to health care for all, who owns and manages the services is a question of secondary importance, although it may be necessary to set strict rules of competition. In Canada for example the government has prohibited insurers offering services provided by the public scheme. On the other hand, in a narrower comparison of 'planned market' experiments in Northern Europe, Saltmann and Von Otter (1992) believe there are significant advantages to be gained by limiting competition to public providers, rather than having a mixed market of public and private competitors as in the UK.

A commitment to social learning would have implications for the role of the Department of Health and NHS Management Executive as well. They would have an important responsibility in creating the conditions in which learning can take place (for example, investments in training), undertaking and disseminating research on technology assessment, clinical outcomes, quality assurance and good management practice (including developing codes of managerial ethics).

The most important task of government is to set the value framework and show the consistency of purpose which alone can bring about progress on the route to Health for All. Although derived from the private sector, Peters and Waterman's 'loose–tight' metaphor seems most appropriate here. They argued that excellent companies granted considerable autonomy to their subsidiaries and staff, but were fanatical in their insistence that the mission and core values of the organisation permeated all its activities, and that staff incorporated those values through training and management development. Managers are held to account for a few key indicators of performance.

In the NHS, however the actions of ministers too often breach their publicly stated values, performance measures are still too diffuse and contradictory and real autonomy is thwarted by the weight of centralised accountability upward. Although the reforms, coupled with the revolution in information technology, suggest how the centralisation–decentralisation paradox may be resolved, in practice the NHS still behaves like a bureaucratic hierarchy in spite of the commitment spelt out in WFP to decentralisation and devolution. In the end the future of the NHS is bound up with Britain's political will and economic fortunes and it is far from clear how these will develop in the run-up to the twenty-first century. What is very clear, however, is that the pace of change will not abate. To survive and prosper the NHS must develop a learning culture. If it can succeed it could be as admired a model for the future as it has been in the past.

If it fails to do so there is another, sadder, scenario: a more expensive, fragmented and inequitable system, where trusts and GP fundholders are the major players, and DHAs are left with a residual role. The promise of the new public health is lost, inequalities widen and 'Health of the Nation' is no more than an historical footnote. What a pity it will be if Britain fails to catch the moment and grasp the opportunity to build a health service which really addresses the needs of the 1990s and beyond.

References

Ashburner, L. and Cairncross, L. (1992) 'Just trust us', *Health Service Journal*, 14 May: 20–22.

Cochrane, A. (1986) 'Community politics and democracy' in D. Held and C. Pollitt (eds) *New Forms of Democracy*, London: Sage/Open University.

—(1992) 'Is there a future for local government?', *Critical Social Policy,* 35: 4–19.

Croft, S. and Beresford, P. (1992) 'The politics of participation', *Critical Social Policy*, 35: 20–44.

East Anglian Regional Health Authority/Office for Public Management (1992) *The Rubber Windmill '92: Planning to Achieve Health Gain*, Cambridge: EARHA/OPM.

Elstad, J.I. 'Health service and decentralised government: the case of primary health services in Norway', *International Journal of Health Sciences*, 20 (4): 545–59.

Glennerster, H., Matsaganis, M. and Owens, P. (1992) *A Foothold for Fundholding*, Research Report 12, London: King's Fund Institute.

Ham, C. (1992) *Locality Purchasing*, Discussion Paper 30, Birmingham: Health Services Management Centre, University of Birmingham.

Ham, C., Robinson, R. and Benzeval, M. (1990) *Health Check*, London: King's Fund Institute.

Hancock, T. (1991) 'National and international health goals and healthy public policy', in P. Draper (ed) Health through public policy, London: Merlin Press.

Hurst, J. and Poullier, J. (1993) *The Reform of Health Care Systems: A Comparative Analysis of Seven OECD Countries*, Paris: OECD.

Lewis, N. and Longley, D. (1993) 'Accountability in education, social services and health' in *Accountability to the Public*, London: European Policy Forum.

Loughton, D. (1992) 'Providing efficient health care for the future' in *Advancing the Health Reforms*, London: Institute of Health Service Management.

Maynard, A. (1991) 'Will competition work?' in *Internalising the Market: Quality, Information and Choice*, London: Institute of Health Service Management.

McKinlay, J.B. and Stoeckle, J. (1988) 'Corporatization and the social transformation of doctoring', *International Journal of Health Services*, 18 (2): 191–203.

Morgan, G. (1986) *Images of Organisation*, London: Sage.

Parston, G. (1991) 'Intentions and possibilities in the commissioning process' in *Beyond the Contract Relationship*, London: Institute of Health Service Management.

Peters, T.J. and Waterman, R.H. (1982) *In Search of Excellence, Lessons from America's Best Run Companies*, New York: Harper and Row.

Ranade, W. (1993) 'Cultural change in the NHS', Paper prepared for meeting of the Comparative Health Policy Study Group, International Political Studies Association, The Hague, Netherlands.

Rathwell, T. (1992) 'A voice in the wilderness', *Health Service Journal* 29 Oct: 21.

Saltmann, R.B. and Von Otter, C. (1992) *Planned Markets and Public Competition*, Buckingham: Open University Press.

Stewart, J. (1993) 'The rebuilding of public accountability', in *Accountability to the Public*, London: European Policy Forum.

Stewart, J. and Stoker, G. (eds) (1989) *The Future of Local Government*, Basingstoke: Macmillan Education.

Tomlinson, Sir B. (1992) *Report of the Inquiry into London's health service, medical education and research*, London: Department of Health.

Winkler, F. (1991) 'Commissioning and the consumer', in *Beyond the Contract Relationship*, London: Institute of Health Service Management.

Appendix – Quality of Service Specification 1992/93 Headings

1   Statement of aims and purpose

2   Quality standards:
    for example, 'The Purchaser requires the provider to have broad-
    based standards for health care services (defined at an agreed level
    of performance within available resources) by patient or speciality
    group, known and understood by all staff within the following
    timetable:'

3   Adherence to statutory and other national codes of practice:
    for example, adherence to employment legislation, health and safety
    at work, environmental health standards, fire regulations, and so on,
    plus district policies on non-smoking, spinal awareness, locally
    agreed arrangements for interagency cooperation for the protection
    of children from abuse, and so on.

4   Quality improvements 1992–93:
    ● waiting list management:
      for example 'With effect from 1 April 1992 all new patients
      must receive confirmation that they have been put on an
      inpatient or outpatient waiting list and the guaranteed date by
      which they will be admitted for their particular treatment'.
    ● admission arrangement (inpatients) including day surgery:
      for example, 'Admission units should endeavour to offer
      accommodation for relatives of patients admitted with a serious
      condition, if required. Where patients are in hospital with a life-
      threatening condition, accommodation should be provided for
      next of kin if requested'.

5   Waiting time for initial consultation, diagnosis and treatment:
    for example, 'The Provider should ensure as far as practicable that out-
    patient clinics start on time, in accordance with the clinic schedule'.

6   Theatre utilisation:
    for example, 'Clear policies are expected on the appropriate staffing
    levels and skill mix to support the most efficient and effective use
    of operating departments'.

7   Discharge arrangements:
    for example, 'The Provider should ensure that wards and
    departments have up-to-date discharge procedures agreed with those
    within and outside the district who will be involved in their
    implementation'.

8   Patients dying in hospital:
    for example, 'Local guidelines on dealing with patients who die in
    hospital (in line with Circular HSG(92)8 requirements) are
    operational and well understood by all staff involved'.

9 Health promotion and disease prevention:
includes a requirement to implement district health promotion policies on smoking, food, alcohol; participate in inter-agency health promotion work; client education; health promotion for staff, and so on.

10 Improvements in personal care services and the Patient's Charter (sets out the Patient's Charter standards to be implemented by agreement by April 1992 plus locally required improvements): for example, 'The Provider should ensure that arrangements are in place to have access to or employ specialist staff who can provide nutritional support, for whatever individual or group of patients who require it'.

11 Audit:
requirement that medical, nursing, paramedical and psychology, and management audit systems are in place, and what information the Purchaser would expect access to: for example, 'The Purchaser expects to receive a summary of audit work being undertaken in each speciality within the unit'.

12 Processes and outcomes:
includes information pertaining to health care quality required for monitoring purposes on a bimonthly basis for
● general and legal complaints, incidents and service complaints;
● major clinical incidents, for example, equipment failure, injury to patients or staff, drug mishaps;
● incidence of hospital acquired infection;
● incidence of pressure sores;
● information on waiting lists, by speciality;
● specific outcome or quality standards information agreed in individual contracts.

INDEX